P9-BJL-669

A Wealth of Voices:

The Edmonton Social Planning Council
1940 - 1990

by
Marsha Mildon

Acknowledgements
   The Edmonton Social Planning Council is grateful for the financial contribution received from the United Way of Edmonton and the Clifford E. Lee Foundation to assist with the publication of this book.

PRINTED IN CANADA

Canadian Cataloguing in Publication Data

Mildon, Marsha, 1946—
   A wealth of voices

ISBN 0921417-00-4

   1. Edmonton Social Planning Council—History.
   2. Edmonton (Alta.)—Social policy—History.
   I. Edmonton Social Planning Council.   II. Title.
   HN110.E35M5 1990   361.2'5'09712334   C90-091708-3
                          71621

Cover Design: Vern Busby

Table of Contents

Preface

The opportunity to write the history of the first fifty years of the Edmonton Social Planning Council's existence was mentioned to me in September 1989, in a casual meeting in a restaurant. Instantly, I was excited by the prospect and spent most of that day's lunch scribbling down ideas and memories that might be part of such a book. The actual project began in January 1990. I have spent the last six months engrossed in the history of an agency which is really a history of social development in Edmonton, since the Council has both led and been part of the social development of this city and province.

It is not a unitary story. Every person I interviewed and every publication, letter, and set of Board Minutes I read, has told its own story. The story of the Council is the sum of many stories and many voices speaking those stories. In discussing myth, Claude Levi-Strauss suggests that we must abandon a search for the one "true" version, and instead "define the myth as consisting of all its versions" (The Time Falling Bodies Take To Light). I believe the same to be true of history, at least, of the history of the Council. Its strength has been in the very variety of those who have supported it over fifty years; its strength is also in the diversity of its actions and its ability to recognize and adapt to changes in the social, economic, and political environment.

While accepting the wealth of stories I have received, I have tried to be as accurate as possible with all the particulars. Any errors of fact must be laid at my door. More difficult, for me, has been the necessity to select which stories to tell. The very richness of the Council's history has made it necessary to leave out several of its projects, and even more of the people who have had a part in it. Throughout, I wished it could be otherwise, but short of writing several volumes, it was inevitable. As much as possible I have tried to let the voices of each era of the Council speak for themselves. I owe a great deal to all those who patiently allowed me to interview them, to the Edmonton City Archives staff who allowed me to roam at will through the 32 boxes of Planning Council files, and to all the current staff and my editorial committee at the Edmonton Social Planning Council. Thank you.

—Marsha Mildon

Section One

1939 – 49:
The Pioneer Years

Chapter One

A Great Day for Edmonton

"This is a great day for Edmonton!" With these words, the *Edmonton Journal* announced that 50 social agencies had voted to create the Edmonton Council of Social Agencies. It was Tuesday evening, June 27, 1939. The place was the MacDonald Hotel. The exuberant speaker was John Blue, secretary-manager of the Edmonton Chamber of Commerce. The vote that evening was the culmination of over a decade of spade work by many Edmonton citizens; it was also the beginning of a story of idealism, struggle, innovation and determination; the story of the Edmonton Social Planning Council.

The moving spirit that Tuesday evening was John M. Imrie, Managing Editor of the *Edmonton Journal*. Imrie is first noticeable as a major initiator of the Council in March of 1939 when Mr. Philip Fisher, Vice-President of Southam Publishing in Montreal and a member of the Canadian Welfare Council's Board of Governors, visited Edmonton and spoke to the organizing group, started by the Junior Chamber of Commerce. No doubt the Managing Editor of the *Journal*, a Southam paper, was interested to hear the views of one of his bosses. Certainly, by April, Imrie was very much involved. He personally called an informal dinner meeting at the MacDonald Hotel, on Friday, April 21, 1939, for specially invited social agency representatives and interested individuals.

Guest List For Dinner and Informal Discussion re Council of Social Agencies in Edmonton invited by John Imrie, held at Mac-Donald Hotel, Friday, April 21, 1939

Mrs. John Gillespie, Mrs. Hugh A. Black, Mrs. R.C. Marshall, Mrs. H. A. Friedman, Mrs. Marion Conroy, Mrs. T.H. Field, Mrs. P. R. Gaboury, Mrs. Ranald D. White, Miss Isabel Munro, Col. T.C. Sims, Rev. Canon C.F.A. Clough, Dr. R.T. Washburn, Hon. J.F. Lymburn, K.C., Mr. John Blue, Robert Chapman,

Mr. J. Gordon Butler, M.C. Fraser. Dr. H. E. Smith, L. Lloyd Jones, C.D. Mackenzie, Clyde Hooke, R.H. Settle, James Walker, H. Radcliffe, Rev. Father T. Ryan, Mr. J.K. Hill, Mr. J.H. Wildman, Mr. H.H. Cooper, and Rev. J.T. Stephens (ESPC Files, City of Edmonton Archives)

Imrie must have been a man of strong motivational talent, the sort who could describe a concept to others and excite them. His letters indicate he was passionate about the need for a Council, but keenly aware of the difficulties. From his Journal office on Friday, April 21, he wrote to Marjorie Bradford, Executive Assistant, at the Canadian Welfare Council describing his anticipation of the evening's dinner meeting:

Tonight is our meeting and I am looking forward to it hopefully, although a bit anxiously. So many previous attempts in Edmonton along similar lines have failed that I must not allow myself to be too optimistic about tonight. But excellent background work has been done at the two meetings which Mr. Philip Fisher addressed and in private conversations since. Then too, the need of something more definite, more comprehensive, and more efficient than exists in Edmonton today is being recognized by an ever widening circle. (ESPC Files, City of Edmonton Archives)

Imrie's background work had been well done; the meeting was a success. In fact, there had been background work done by many people since the late 1920's.

As early as 1927, there were people in Edmonton who felt a need for an organization to co-ordinate social service work. On February 4, 1927, the Edmonton Journal reported:

The names of Mrs. Arthur Murphy and Bishop Gray, as vice presidents of the Social Services Board of Northern Alberta have been added to the list of officers, with His Honour Lieutenant Governor Egbert as patron, His Grace, Bishop O'Leary as honorary president, Mrs. W.R. Howey, secretary, and Ald. C.L. Gibbs as treasurer.

In order to enlist as wide a circle of interest as possible in the movement for social services, the board will also add to itself two representatives from each city church, one representative from each service club, one from the board of trade, Salvation Army, women's organizations and other clubs.

This committee, formed as a kind of branch of the Canadian Council of Child Welfare (shortly to become the Canadian Welfare Council), met several times through 1928 and 1929. There were other such committees and other nascent Councils springing up across the country. The impetus seems to have been a new awareness of child welfare needs after the First World War. The Edmontonians wanted to know what others were doing and to be part of that national movement. However, their firm conviction was that their city required a community chest to do joint fund-raising, and that this might well solve their social service problems, without the necessity of a Council. The social service community across the country disagreed.

In May, 1929, J. Howard Falk, Executive Director of the Montreal Council, came to Edmonton and spoke to the committee and other service clubs. His message was first of all a message about the true nature of social work as opposed to mere "relief":

> Three pertinent points in the development of a community chest for Edmonton charities were outlined by J. Howard T. Falk . . . Tuesday night.

> The first of these points was that proper social work does not stop with the clothing, feeding and housing of a neglected child. The youngster must be educated and developed so he will become an independent citizen rather than a burden. (*The Edmonton Journal*, May 29, 1929)

Falk's second two points concerned the care and planning which was required in forming any sort of co-ordinating body for social services, as a false start was often worse than no start at all. His advice was to conduct a careful survey of the social services in the city in order to ascertain what existed, what was needed, and to recommend the best way in which to proceed. The committee agreed and promptly requested Falk to do the survey. Ultimately, Marjorie Bradford, Falk's assistant in Montreal was hired to do the survey under Falk's supervision.

Bishop Grey headed up the survey committee, and John Blue, then secretary of the Chamber of Commerce was also secretary of the committee. The survey was to be thorough, dealing with "the dependent family; the dependent individual; the homeless transient; the dependent child or children; the unmarried mother and child; the dependent sick and convalescent sick; and the insane." (*The Edmonton Journal*, August 2, 1929).

Completing her work by September, Bradford found many instances of overlapping as well as gaps in services and recommended that a council of community services and, even more important, a family welfare bureau were needed in Edmonton long before a community chest could be organized to do joint fund-raising. She was a woman of strong convictions. When the idea of a community chest reappeared in 1936, she repeated her rejection of the notion that a community chest should be organized first in a letter replying to Mary (Mrs. John) Gillespie's query on the subject:

One remark in your letter (about the panacea for financial troubles) recalls the two most current misunderstandings I encountered when I did the Edmonton study. One was that the community chest was a panacea for all the financial troubles of the individual agency and by some magic could suddenly produce all their requirements out of a hat. The other was that the community chest centralizes everything; - abolishes the autonomy of the individual agencies and heads up all activities in one central office. This, of course, appealed to some business elements in the community and decidedly did not appeal to the agencies concerned. I tried to set them straight on this second point and spent some considerable time and effort endeavouring to show them how the financial success of a community chest must be built. For instance, the very best foundation on which the financial success of a community chest can be laid is a basic list of regular and interested subscribers to the societies who will join in the community chest. When those societies have built up a good subscription lists (sic) and interested bodies of supporters through direct contacts and appeals, it is so much easier to get a community chest going, but as I pointed out in Edmonton, a great deal of their money raising was by indirect methods. A tremendous amount of effort was put into the organization of tag days, concerts, bazaars, and all those things, and the people whose support was secured through those means, for the most part developed no direct contact with the appealing agency. Moreover, as an instance of results, as I remember it, it required fourteen tag days in Edmonton to raise $7,000 in the twelve months preceding our study and as we pointed out in the report, when a man or woman has contributed to fourteen tag days, they have a feeling that they have given a lot of money to charity although trifling amounts have been involved.(ESPC Files, City of Edmonton Archives)

Bishop Gray's committee accepted the report and would likely have proceeded with the development of a Council, but the stock market crash on black Tuesday, October 29, 1929 interrupted their plans and heralded the Depression that would change the face of social services in Canada.

Despite the Depression, the idea of organizing a community chest kept recurring. In 1936, the individual agencies could not raise enough money to meet their own needs. A group of citizens headed by Father Ryan suggested that a community chest, collecting for all agencies together, might solve the problem. This group, however, also disappeared, and it was left to a group from the Junior Chamber of Commerce, led by Robert Chapman, to raise the issue again in 1939. Marjorie Bradford, in her characteristically direct style, describes these early attempts in letters to Phillip Fisher, briefing him before his March 1939 visit to Edmonton:

> The latest movement to form a Community Chest seems to have arisen about two years ago, and Miss Whitton [Executive Director of Canadian Welfare Council], who visited all the western centres at the time of our regional conferences out there, found herself addressing meetings and taking part in discussions which were chiefly concerned with some sort of mixture of a Community Chest and a Social Service Exchange.

> The chief protagonist of the Community Chest idea at the time was Father Ryan, a young and active priest who, I think, had not been so very long in Edmonton. His sponsorship of this idea did not seem to take very much note of the real job to be done in Edmonton on social service co-ordination, and also it seemed somewhat unfortunate that the chief agitation for the whole thing should be coming from one of a minority religious group in Edmonton. There was a feeling that the Catholics would probably be getting a lot more out of it than they would be putting in, and they have some very large Catholic institutions there, which ought to be partly emptied no doubt rather than strengthened with too much support. Whatever the merits of Father Ryan's idea, I think it is a foregone conclusion, from my knowledge of Edmonton, that the leadership should be lodged elsewhere and the sponsorship made more representative.

Perhaps that is what is behind the recent move to have the Junior Chamber of Commerce take it up. There again, of course, there may be a danger. I do not think the Junior Chamber has been in existence very long in Edmonton, and I do not know what standing it has achieved and how seriously it is taken. Certainly the Senior Board has doddered along ineffectively on some of those things it has attempted to sponsor in past years, and it may be that the younger group in Edmonton will be the ones to get action, as has been the case to such an extent in Winnipeg. (ESPC Files, City of Edmonton Archives)

Whatever the motivations and rivalries among the earlier groups, John Imrie seems to have been able to incite enthusiasm and co-operation among invitees to his dinner. On April 24, 1939 he wrote to Marjorie Bradford:

You will be pleased to learn that the dinner meeting on the 21st inst. accomplished all that could have been expected of it.

Following my own introductory talk there was a general discussion in which most of the twenty-eight present participated. This discussion revealed recognition of the need of a Council of Social Agencies, a Family Welfare Bureau, and a Social Service Exchange, to a much greater degree than I had anticipated. It is true that several said their recognition of such need had come to them only as the discussion progressed. One man, for instance, declared that if asked twenty-four hours earlier he would have answered in the negative a question as to such need; but now after hearing my statement and the first hour of discussion he saw the need as very, very great.

Finally, the meeting put through two resolutions by unanimous vote. One endorsed the idea of the early establishment of the three organizations in question. The other invited me to take the initiative in convening a fourth meeting consisting this time of accredited representatives of a selected list of social service agencies about whose right to inclusion in a Council of Social Agencies there could be no question. (ESPC Files, City of Edmonton Archives)

The fourth meeting was somewhat delayed because Imrie was busy putting out a Royal Edition of the Journal to celebrate the visit of Their Majesties. However, he and Miss Bradford continued to correspond, and she continued to advise him on tactics for organizing:

Possibly at your first [fourth] meeting another good thing to do might be to have one or two of your existing welfare agencies interpret some of the needs for coordination and for a follow-up family welfare service in Edmonton. Usually you can count on your Victorian Order Nurse to offer some excellent interpretation on this subject, and I think the Victoria Order in Edmonton is quite interested and wants to be helpful. (ESPC Files, City of Edmonton Archives, May 17, 1939)

It would be as well to plan from the beginning not to have your group too over-weighted with women, but to devise ways and means of bringing in at least an equal number of men if you can. Later on the proportions will not matter much, but in the beginning if you do not watch that point the men are likely to leap quickly to the conclusion that this is a woman's affair, and it is hard to break down an initial impression of that sort. It might be that you could overcome the difficulty by agreeing in the very beginning to add a limited number of individual members (not in a representative capacity) to your Council, and then you could draw in some good leadership that way. (ESPC Files, City of Edmonton Archives, June 8, 1939)

The fourth meeting was finally held on Tuesday, June 13, 1939. The agency representatives agreed to take the proposal back to their Board's and to return two weeks later for a vote on the proposal. On June 27, 1939, the vote was affirmative; the initiation phase was over; the formation began.

By this time, John Imrie had a clear plan in mind for the development of his organization, but still he wrote to Bradford for concurrence:

The resolution to be submitted calls for the appointment of a committee of nine, selected by the chairman, to raise the necessary funds. I hope to have acceptances by Tuesday night from those I would like to see on that committee and thus be able to announce immediately its personnel.

This committee will consist of people who are known to be good at raising money irrespective of their past association with specific social service agencies. I hope to persuade Mr. W.T. Henry to accept the chairmanship. He is one of our most respected citizens, was mayor for three years, is an excellent organizer, and his name as chairman would facilitate the raising of the money.

It seems to me there should be another committee composed of leaders in social service work for collaboration with whoever will conduct the survey. Do you agree as to this? I have in mind consultation in a day or two with Mrs. John Gillespie and one or two other social service leaders as to the best personnel for this committee. My own thought at the moment is that its personnel should be non-professional; what is your judgment as to that?

In talks to the large meeting one week ago and to several clubs meanwhile, I suggested that the survey should commence on or about Sept. 1st, would occupy about three months, and that it might be Jan. 1st, next before the Council of Social Agencies and the two subsidiary organizations would be functioning on a permanent basis. (ESPC Files, City of Edmonton Archives, June 20, 1939)

With Bradford's blessing, and the approval of the agencies, the process moved ahead. Under W.T. Henry's chairmanship, the finance committee began their fund-raising, while the social service committee hired Laura Holland, from Vancouver, to do a survey of needs and an outline of how best to begin the organization.

Miss Holland C.B.E. (Commander of the Order of the British Empire) had long experience in social work. She had been head of the Division of Social Welfare of the City of Toronto before she came to the position of Secretary of the Children's Aid Society of Vancouver. Later, she became Provincial Superintendent of Child Welfare in British Columbia. In 1939, although she was also Chief Inspector under the new Welfare Institutions Licensing Act in Vancouver, she was convalescing from ill health, and a temporary job such as the survey in Edmonton was exactly what she wanted. She began in September and delivered her report, by mail, in December.

The report indicated that over $160,000 was spent by the major private social service agencies in 1938:

Of this amount, approximately $105,000 was contributed voluntarily by generous citizens, and $55,000 was revenue or earned income - i.e., fees for club activities, board paid by parents or relatives or some department of government . . . . During the same year the Federal, Provincial and Municipal governments have expended over $1,000,000 on relief alone in the city area. (Holland, 1939)

In addition to surveying the financial status of social services and the actual work done by the forty-seven agencies which she surveyed, Miss Holland also gave a brief review of how social service had changed since the first World War, creating the need for new organizations like the Council-to-be:

Throughout Canada, during the past twenty years, public interest in the 'social services' has steadily increased with the recognition that the 'neighbourliness' and methods of pioneer days are neither adequate nor possible under the complex modern conditions of an urban centre. (Holland, 1939)

She acknowledged that the Depression created needs that were well "beyond the ability of 'private charity' alone and 'relief' became to a greater extent than ever before the accepted responsibility of governments and the taxpayer." However, after pointing out that the agency — in this case the government — responsible for giving relief should also provide case work support, she went on to explain the need for the continuance of private agencies:

But there are many maladjusted individuals and families who are emotionally unstable who are not eligible for public assistance nor perhaps in need of it but who may later become permanent public charges unless helped to overcome their attitude of defeatism, inferiority or disillusionment. It is to deal with such situations that Family Welfare or Service Bureaus under private auspices have been, and are being organized in many communities. In such an agency, each family or person is treated individually. A diagnosis of the problem is made on the basis of the personal or family history obtained and the knowledge gained of the character, habits and attitude of the individuals involved. A plan of treatment is undertaken in which the client is a partner, and as required the co-operation is sought of agencies, equipped to give special services such as child care, medical aid, recreation and even material relief when this is necessary for treatment. (Holland, 1939)

Holland's report recommended the immediate formation of a Council of Social Agencies with an associated Social Services Exchange to assist agencies in determining whether they were providing services to clients who used several agencies, and a Family Service Bureau to provide professional casework to families and children in need.

While Holland was at work on her survey, the rest of Imrie's committee continued work on the organizational process. John Imrie himself became ill towards the end of 1939 and took an enforced vacation to California for his health. On November 30, 1939, William Henry sent the good news of the organization to his old friend:

It is all over. We are now functioning as a full fledged Council of Social Agencies with its allied Family Welfare Bureau and Social Service Index.

Had the final meeting Monday night which passed the constitution and by-laws, appointed the officers, and set up the executive. At the meeting a formal resolution was passed thanking you for your splendid work in initiating and promoting the movement which led to the setting up of the Council, and it was very enthusiastically concurred in by all the members present, of which there were numbered nearly one hundred. You were elected as First Vice Chairman but I tried my best to get you into the position of Honorary Chairman but some thought I was trying to "crawl out from under" and refused to sanction my proposal.

We have just had our first meeting of the executive and passed some formal resolutions necessary to get the machinery moving, such as banking arrangements, appointing a chairman to the sub-committees, the acceptance of our social workers applications for the position, and other details.

We have secured the services of Miss Lillian Thompson of Vancouver as our worker. She is known to Miss Holland who recommended her very highly. Mr. Nickerson also knows her and he gives her his O.K. We expect her to arrive on January 1st to take over her duties at that time.

Needless to say Miss Holland has made a good impression in Edmonton, especially with the private agencies and with the Public Officials, even our mutual friend Mrs. Hart, who, by the way, is not appointed in any official capacity as yet and "likes it" judging by her attitude, thinks Miss Holland is wonderful. Miss Holland is leaving here on Saturday morning and will send her report back from Vancouver when she completes it.

So far we have not been able to select a Second Vice Chairman. The Committee was appointed at the meeting this afternoon to select a name and report at the next meeting. It is rather important that the proper person is chosen as I will be away for the first few months of the formative period, so that the Second Vice Chairman will have to carry on in my absence. It is therefore very important that the party appointed should be in complete sympathy with the Movement.

I hope you and Mrs. Imrie are enjoying Sunny California and that you are on the road to complete recovery and will be able to return in a few months ready to give another twenty years of public service.

We have not yet made any definite plans for the immediate future but it looks now as though it would be California for three months at least.

With kind personal regards to yourself and Good Wife, I remain.

(ESPC Files, City of Edmonton Archives, November 30, 1939)

Chapter Two

Pioneer Work Under Particularly Good Auspices

When Lillian Thomson arrived in Edmonton on the weekend of January 27, 1940, to take up her position as first Executive Director of the brand new Edmonton Council of Social Agencies, the Executive Committee was enthusiastic. Indeed, since November 30, 1939, when they had received word of her acceptance of the position, they had been waiting impatiently. Telegraphs and night letters had travelled between her office in Vancouver and the Edmonton group urging her to arrive as soon as possible, preferably January 1. There was not, in the Committee's opinion, a moment to lose.

In fact, it was Monday, the 29th of January, 1940, when the Executive Committee welcomed their new employee, listened to her plans for her work, and appointed a committee to find office space. Fortunately, William Henry, chairman of the Council, was a partner in a well-established Edmonton furniture business. By February 1, he and Miss Thomson had not only secured, but furnished an office on the third floor of the Tegler Building. The Council of Social Agencies was in business, albeit a decade later than in many other centres in Canada.

Lillian Thomson was not at all ignorant of the job ahead of her. She had been Assistant Director for the Council of Social Agencies in Vancouver before she came to Edmonton, and had a strong background in family case work. Her friend and colleague, Laura Holland, had written her even before the position was offered to apprise her of the Edmonton situation. Of particular note, and repeated in several letters by Holland, was the lack of any 'modern' case work being done with families and the lack of good child welfare services. On the bright side stood the enthusiasm and good will of those involved in developing the Council, and the generosity of the community.

By the time Thomson arrived, the work of the Council was already well underway. The Executive Committee consisted of well-placed representatives of business, law, medicine, social welfare services, and the church, and included such influential people as Cora Casselman, soon to be a Member of Parliament, and Elmer Roper, soon to be an MLA, and later to be Mayor of Edmonton. The Constitution, passed at the meeting on November 30, 1939, and officially incorporated July 4, 1940, listed three Objects of the Council which were typical of the main elements of social service thinking of the time:

The new Council was well supported financially by the Edmonton community as reported in the Executive Committee's minutes:

The Following Subscriptions are for Three Years

Northwestern Utilities	500.00
Edmonton Journal	250.00
Private Citizen	150.00
Johnstone-Walker Ltd.	100.00
Taylor & Pearson	100.00
Edmonton Bulletin per C. Campbell	100.00
Crown Paving Co.	100.00
King Edward Hote	150.00
Royal George Hote	150.00
Selkirk & Yale Hotels Per. Mrs. MacDonald	50.00
H.G. McDonald	50.00
Blowey Henry Ltd.	50.00
McGavin's Bakery	50.00
John Gillespie	100.00
Edmonton Credit Co.	50.00
Weber Bros.	50.00
Huff Investment	25.00
Elmer Roper	10.00
D. M. Duggan	25.00
North West Brewing	100.00
Edmonton Brewery	100.00
Western Supplies	10.00
Crescent Furniture Co.	25.00
Campbell Furniture Co.	10.00
H. Tait Groceries	25.00
Provincial News	15.00
Great West Garment	25.00
Marshall Wells Alta. Ltd.	100.00
Canadian Pacific Co. Per. A.W. Neal	100.00

C. Woodward Ltd.	100.00
Capitol Theatre	25.00
Calgary Power Co.	50.00
Total	$2545.00

In addition, the Junior Chamber of Commerce had collected pledges of another $165/year for three years, and the committee had collected a further $2525 for the first year of operation. Their goal had been to begin with $6000 in hand. Out of this, $2400/year was salary for Thomson, and as pointed out to her, again by letter from Laura Holland,

There is no mincing the fact that your salary will be looked upon as a large one, but I think that has been true whenever a professional person has pioneered in a field in most cities and usually it is lived down, meanwhile making a definite contribution to the profession concerned. (ESPC Files, City of Edmonton Archives, November 9 1939)

All indications are that Thomson did live up to expectations and "live down" her large salary. Studies and reports soon began to flow from the four Divisions — Family, Children, Health, and Group Work — into which the Council was organized.

These Divisions were made up of representatives from each member agency in the particular interest area. Their duties, as laid out in the Constitution, were as follows:

(a) to consider and report on matters specifically referred to them by the Executive Committee;
(b) to study and gather data upon general problems arising from time to time within their respective fields;
(c) to refer to the Executive Committee special problems uncovered in the course of their investigations which do not lie within their particular field but may be more adequately handled by some other committee. (Article 19)

The Divisions were required by the Constitution to meet at least four times yearly. In fact, they plunged into their work. A typical Division meeting was that of the Health Division, held at the University Hospital Out-Patients' Clinic on the evening of October 22, 1940. There were sixteen people present representing the Civic Board of Health, the Registered Nurses' Association, the Victorian Order of Nurses, St. John Ambulance Association, the Junior Hospital League, University Hospital Auxiliary, the University Hospital Out-Patients'

Department, and the Council of Social Agencies, as well as a guest architect from the Town Planning Commission. A sense of the seriousness with which they took their work and the range of their concerns can be inferred from the report of their discussions.

The meeting began with a report on plans for classes to be given to mothers on subjects such as pre-natal care, child care, nutrition, and the sewing of baby clothes. The next report was on requests by various groups for information on nutrition and the appointment of a representative to the Family Welfare Division to make suggestions regarding Christmas hampers. Then, Dr. Little, of the Civic Board of Health, launched into a discussion of housing, based on a small survey done by the Board. Before going further, he requested that

> there should be no publicity regarding the report and subsequent discussion at this meeting. (Minutes, Health Division, Oct. 22, 1940)

The problems he described were many:

> The survey revealed rooming houses numbering 103 to be in a state of poor preservation. The Provincial Government allowance of ten cents a night per individual, led to overcrowding. While not included in the Survey, families renting rooms for light-housekeeping also reduced costs at the expense of adequate space, so that as many as ten person to a room have been noted. Many private homes have taken in one or more families to increase income, with no structural alteration in the dwelling.

Dr. Little went on to comment that the increasing population of the city through the 1930's and the tax rates were adding to the problems of insufficient housing, unaffordable housing, and substandard housing:

> The advertising columns in newspapers do not list many houses. The conclusion is there is very little unoccupied accommodation in Edmonton, especially for families with children and on low incomes.

> Many houses and shacks used for dwellings should be condemned, but there is no other room for the residents. Communicable disease is thus spread and social proprieties violated.

The discussion continued at length as Division members brought up examples of housing solutions such as the Swedish "magic houses" [prefabs] financed by the Swedish government and a co-operative association in Trail B.C. which administered a housing program. Before the meeting adjourned, the architect, Professor Cecil Burgess of the Town Planning Commission, encouraged the Division members to carry out a sound statistical survey of housing on which action could be based, and a committee was set up to do so. It is quite possible to imagine the participants walking out of the hospital late on that October evening, still talking with each other, indignant about the situation of the ill-housed and eager to begin working towards solutions. Clearly, the Health Division did not see itself limited to a narrow definition of health as matters of medical care only.

In fact, it was obvious by the time of the first annual general meeting, held in the Jasper Room of the MacDonald Hotel on February 7, 1941, that no part of the new Council took a narrow view of its work. The prime purpose of the organization, certainly from the point of view of many of the organizers, was to improve the efficiency of 'relief' services through co-operation and co-ordination. But the needs that quickly became apparent to all, along with the overwhelming influence of the first year of World War II, led Council members to view their work as an essential aspect of democracy. The opening to the Annual Report expresses the intensity and importance of this realization:

Events of staggering import in Canada and throughout the world provided the backdrop for the first year's work of the Edmonton Council of Social Agencies. After winter months of ominous quiet, the word 'Blitzkrieg' overnight took on a grim clarity of meaning. Denmark — Norway — Holland — Belgium — France — and with the autumn the most ferocious aerial assault in the history of warfare was launched against Britain. Total war had come. This Dominion too had elected to fight. By the end of the year Canadians had grimly adopted two resolutions: They would protect the machinery of democracy with their lives in Dover or Iceland or any other theatre of war. They would at last accept the seriousness of their task as guardians of that machinery at home and make themselves competent in its modern use instead of regarding it as a precious but cumbersome heirloom. By the first resolution, the rank and file of Canadians simply mean that the war will be won. By the second, they mean that they will make democracy work. They will make democracy work in the

daily lives of common citizens, in their free, confident association with each other, and in their acceptance of personal responsibility for the common good. It was against this national
backdrop, built of physical challenge and moral determination,
that Edmonton's welfare organizations had their first year's
experience in co-operative association.

It was clear from the Annual Report that each of the Divisions had
moved with enthusiasm and vision into their acceptance of responsibility for the common good.

The Health Division had its nutrition and parent education classes
underway; a Layette Exchange had been organized to prevent duplication in the provision of layettes for needy mothers; the Housing
Committee had been formed, and discussion of the need for social
services in hospitals had begun. As a matter of policy, members of
the Health Division made it clear that they saw

"that much medical work is wasted effort because of poor social
conditions in the homes and that a constructive social program
[was] urgently needed".

The Child Welfare Division had arranged for library service from
the Edmonton Public Library to several of the city's children's institutions; a second committee of nine had begun work surveying the
problems of juvenile delinquency in the city and acting as voluntary
probation officers for delinquents; a third committee had begun the
task of encouraging the formation of Home and School organizations
in Edmonton, with the first launched at Garneau school.

The Group Work Division was particularly active. Perhaps because
the war had already taken many of the up and coming leaders away
from the city, there was a major concern with training community
leadership. Working together over the year, groups such as Boy Scouts,
YMCA, Girl Guides, church youth groups, and the Better Health
Camp Council had organized a leadership training course, a Camp
Institute on various aspect of camping procedure, and planned a survey
of group work services and needs.

The Family Welfare Division was most concerned with co-ordination
of services during that first year of operation, both to conserve
resources, even more precious because of the war effort, and to avoid
"the demoralization that thrives on unnecessary assistance". Representatives of agencies, all concerned with the welfare of families in

their own homes and public or voluntary relief, met to begin the task of building the trust and confidence between agencies necessary to begin tackling the problems of duplication. This Division, more than the others, was closely tied in with the work of the three 'sub-agencies' of the Council: the Social Services Exchange, the Christmas Exchange, and the Family Welfare Bureau.

The creation of the Social Services Exchange and the Family Welfare Bureau were part of the original proposal for the Council. The Social Service Exchange was a card index file in which each member agency would register the names of the families it was assisting. When two or more agencies registered the same family, the Exchange staff would "inform them of their mutual interest" (Annual Report, 1940). Setting up this Exchange was one of the first tasks for Lillian Thomson when she arrived in Edmonton, and while everyone agreed with the idea of avoiding duplication, the practical aspects of the Exchange were not easy to arrange. Agencies were concerned about the possibilities of breaching confidentiality that such an Exchange could allow, and of course, agencies were not completely without certain professional jealousies. Nevertheless, by the Annual Meeting, twenty-five organizations were using the Exchange.

They registered the names of 5,461 families and 555 of these names were found to have been registered previously. In 1,447 instances, participating agencies were informed that other groups were also interested in the families they had registered. (Annual Report, 1940)

The Christmas Exchange, concerned both with avoiding duplication of Christmas hampers and encouraging similarity in hamper content, was organized as a separate committee but closely linked with both the Social Service Exchange and the Family Welfare Division. This Exchange served 54 organizations and answered enquiries about 1405 families in the month before that first Christmas.

Of all the needs in Edmonton, the need for family case work had been identified as the most critical in both the 1929 and 1939 surveys, and it was this need that a Family Welfare Bureau was to fulfil. It began simultaneously, although somewhat informally, with the work of the Council itself through the work of Lillian Thomson in counselling families under the direction of an informal board of ten members. Over the year, Thomson met with 83 families of whom 59 were taken on for some extended work. The problems these families presented included "financial need, threatened or actual dissolution of family ties, unmarried parenthood, mental ill-health, death, imprisonment, mental deficiency". (Annual Report, 1940). In the Annual Report, Thomson refers to the year's work of the Bureau as a "Test Flight" which showed what could possibly be done if the Bureau had its own full-time staff and facilities. This was marked out as an urgent matter to be dealt with in 1941. Again, there was concern that

> the war has created many new and serious strains in family life, and that insofar as these strains are unrelieved, our war effort will be weakened and the aftermath of war will be the more destructive. (Annual Report, 1940).

Finally, the war also encouraged a change in plans in relation to the long proposed Community Chest:

> When the Council was first organized, it was not expected that a Community Chest would be launched for two or three years. Events in 1940 hastened the development. First, the agencies gained rapidly in their ability to work together, thus building a safe foundation for financial federation. Secondly, contributors were growing increasingly restive with the multiplicity of appeals. One justification for their irritation was indicated in a study of local Tag Days, made early in the year by a committee under the chairmanship of Mr. W.J. Dick. It was found that there had been thirty-six tag-days during 1939. Finally and most important of all, the war created many additional appeals for funds and the necessity for unification increased correspondingly. (Annual Report, 1940)

The Council for the Co-ordination of Auxiliary War Services requested the Council of Social Agencies to investigate the immediate organization of a Community Chest. Meetings were held during December of 1940, and at a Council general meeting on January 27, 1941, a unanimous resolution was passed authorizing the Council to develop a Constitution and bring nominations for a Board to a further general meeting. Elmer Roper, then a member of the Executive Committee of the Council of Social Agencies, has expressed the feelings of the community succinctly:

> I was involved in organizing a representative meeting of business people, labor groups and social activists at which the Chest was launched. All concerned had become fed up with the multiplicity

of appeals for charitable purposes. (letter E.E. Roper to M. Mildon, February 28, 1990)

It is clear from the volume of work alone that the strength of the Council in that first year was the good will and hard work of the agency representatives and volunteers supported by Lillian Thomson, a woman of remarkable energy. She attended all Division meetings and took their Minutes, did the work of a case worker for the Family Welfare Bureau, the work of organizer for the Social Services Exchange, as well as the pioneer work of building a brand new organization up to a membership of 62 organizations and supporting the many staff and volunteers of those organizations who would come to the Council offices for advice.

Chapter Three

Recognition of Unmet Needs

Before World War II, and during the Depression, social service programs "both public and private, were primitive, for the most part, non-existent. The war served as a catalyst for bringing about more awareness" of the need in the social welfare field. (Wass, Address to Social Planning Council Annual Meeting, 1980). Public attitudes were changing significantly as to the degree of public responsibility for social welfare. The standards that might be expected by the citizen in terms of housing and income security were rising. The 1943/44 Annual Report of the Canadian Welfare Council highlights this national sense:

> Whatever the differences in the main proposals . . . , they have at least this important characteristic in common: they all proceed on the assumption that we must take a complete and comprehensive look at our Canadian social service structure and integrate our measures, both provincial and Federal, more completely than we have heretofore attempted to do, if we are to achieve a truly Canadian pattern of social security.

An important part of this structuring and integration had to do with working out relationships between government, private social agencies, and charity. Since the thirties, the government had slowly moved into the social welfare field, primarily providing relief for families. During the 1940's, Unemployment Insurance and Family Allowance programs were created by the federal government, and old age pensions became universal. In 1944 in Alberta, the provincial government set up a Department of Public Welfare, separate from the Department of Health for the first time, although still administered by the Minister of Health, W. W. Cross (Wass, 1980).

At the same time, social work, as a profession separate from "good works and charity", was beginning to come of age. There were, at the time of the formation of the Council of Social Agencies, six professional schools of social work, most notably at Montreal, Toronto, and Vancouver. Despite this growth in social work education, many of those hiring for social welfare positions still preferred to hire people such as veterans or ministers of the church, people of good will, but without specific social work qualifications. Needless to say, the professional social workers in this situation took both their work and their qualifications seriously. They believed in scientific case work principles that could be applied to each troubled family or social problem.

As might be expected, then, with several interested parties, including three levels of government as well as private agencies, and professional social workers, all moving into the same expanding field, there was controversy and dispute over who should be involved and what each should be doing. The decade of the forties for the Council of Social Agencies, thus, must be examined within the general milieu of a growing public/private universe of social welfare in Alberta.

It was also an important decade in terms of the development of the Council itself. Under Lillian Thomson's guidance until February, 1944 and then led by Hazeldine Bishop, the Council began developing the patterns of work which would characterize it for the next 50 years. The major contribution of the Council of Social Agencies during the forties was a contribution to the growth of the private social welfare sector in Edmonton. This was already evident in the first year with the development of the Family Welfare Bureau, Social Service Exchange, Christmas Exchange, and the Community Chest in early 1941. This function, that is identifying gaps in the system and assisting in filling them, has continued to be a major role played by the Council throughout its existence.

In 1940, the Health Division had identified the lack of social services in hospitals as an important gap. Under the chairmanship of Dr. Mary Hunter, the Health Division consulted with the hospitals and examined the role of some parallel professions such as that of public health nurse and the social worker in the outside agency. In 1943, a subcommittee including Dr. Hunter, Lillian Thomson, and Helen MacArthur of the School of Nursing at the University Hospital, developed a brief to the Executive Committee of the Edmonton Hospital Board urging the start of a medical social service department in the Royal Alexandra Hospital:

> Everyone connected with hospital service is aware that some
> patients have personal problems affecting their health and medical

treatment. A problem becomes especially important to the hospital if it postpones discharge of a recovered patient or retards recovery or if subsequent to discharge it causes a relapse and a return of the patient to hospital. Such developments indicate waste of expert medical care and of expensive hospital service.

The committee argued for the appointment of a medical social worker on the grounds of financial efficiency and improved patient care, then ended the brief with a plug for the Royal Alex:

We believe that in the Royal Alexandra Hospital the ground is ready for a demonstration of unusual value to the whole of Western Canada. This hospital is ready to develop social service in advance of other hospitals in this and other provinces because of the high standards obtaining in its other services. Unless all departments in a hospital are efficient, a social service program is greatly handicapped from the start. In the Royal Alexandra this condition is amply fulfilled, and in our opinion the addition of a social worker to the staff would complete a hospital program of outstanding merit.

By the end of the year, the Health Division was able to report with satisfaction that the Hospital Board had approved the idea, provided the extra funds, and the Royal Alexandra had hired Mrs. Elizabeth Richardson for the position.

Another example of identifying gaps and sponsoring new agencies also came in 1943, this time from the Group Work Division. This Division had surveyed the city in 1941 to discover which areas experienced the most delinquency. They had then surveyed the high delinquency areas in terms of the number of group facilities for youth and the percentage of youth involved in those groups. They reported a much smaller percentage of involvement in the high delinquency areas. This, along with their continuing involvement in providing leadership training, led them to believe that more group activities would reduce delinquency. At the same time, fuel and food rationing made it difficult to run the traditional summer camps outside the city. Thus the Group Work Division proposed the creation of In-the-city Camps:

[The Leadership Committee of the Group Work Division] made recommendations to the organizations for the recruiting of leadership in the city, for the training of these leaders and for the setting up of city camps during the months of August. As a result of the proposed long summer holidays for the schools an urgent need has arisen for organized recreation during the summer for the young people. (Report of the Special Committee on Leadership, May 6, 1943)

Bill Pettigrew, a member of the Group Work Division and later President of the Council, moved that the Council of Social Agencies arrange for a fund of $1,000 for the establishment and maintenance of six city camps, and this was approved. The six camps began operating in August, 1943. Pettigrew recounts the beginning of his own work with the Council and particularly the beginning of the Group Work Division's priority, leadership work:

"I was with the Y, and in the church and Tuxis and CGIT, so I got involved through participating in the Council on behalf of the different organizations I was in . . . . I don't know why but I always got to be chairman of whatever I was involved in. We had some great people working there, . . . a big Council. I used to give lessons in leading sing songs and that kind of thing. That was one of those things I liked to do, being Irish, you know.

That [leadership training] was one of the things we tried to do because when we started there were so many people involved who hadn't had any training in how to go about chairing a meeting and that kind of thing." (Interview, Bill Pettigrew, February 28, 1990.)

In addition to its work of promoting leadership and the In-City camps of the private agencies, the Group Work Division was deeply involved in the developing relationships between public and private organizations through its study of recreation undertaken in 1945:

The Group Work Division has been actively supporting the development of publicly financed, properly supervised playgrounds and neighbourhood centres, and it is following with keen interest the progress of the Civic Recreation Commission's plans. It is obvious, however, that public recreation will not, for many years to come — if ever — be able to meet all the leisure time needs of the community, and that existing private organizations can and should be doing a bigger job. But — it is also most important that they should move into those areas where the need is greatest, and that there should not be competition and overlapping in their development. While considerable information about various sections of the City has been collected by the Recreation Commission, and by the School Boards and City Departments, and certain other organizations, nowhere is a complete picture of the City's recreation needs and resources available. This Council, therefore, with the assured co-operation of the Recreation Commission, School Boards, private agencies and others, has undertaken to try to get this over-all picture, the findings to be available to all interested to serve as a guide in working out their plans to the end that these might form part of a coordinated whole. (Annual Report, 1945)

To conduct this study, the Council created a questionnaire regarding recreational activities which was administered by school teachers to Grades 4 to 12 of both the public and separate school systems. Sixteen thousand questionnaires were sent out; 11,373 were returned in usable form. The Council also gathered statistics on juvenile crime from May 1, 1945 to April 30, 1946 to determine delinquency rates, and on the number of persons receiving some form of income support from government to determine dependency rates. The city was divided into 22 recreational districts based on community league boundaries and all the statistical data was organized by district. Then, the Council determined priority of need for additional recreation services in each of the 22 areas by comparing the difference in each area between the average of the delinquency and dependency ranks and the participation rank. This was a massive job of statistical tabulation undertaken by an organization with a staff of one social worker/executive director and volunteers as reported in the Executive Director's address to the 1945 Annual Meeting:

We are on our way — on this big and important job — and with the help of crews working three nights a week, we are starting to tabulate the returns from our first questionnaire — 16,000 of them! It will take time, — considerable time, before the whole survey is complete — but we are confident that getting the facts about our Community is a necessary prerequisite to planning.

In fact, Part I of the *Survey of Recreation in Edmonton* was not actually published until the Annual Meeting of 1947 due primarily to lack of staff resources. It did, however, accomplish its goal of identifying those areas which should be considered priorities in future recreational planning.

Despite the Survey and many briefs and presentations to the City, the question of "how to achieve better integration of public recreation programmes — sponsored by the Civic Recreation Commission — with those of the many private recreation and group work organizations in the City" was still a matter of concern by the end of the decade as was clearly pointed out in the 1949 Annual Report:

> Various proposals have been advanced from time to time, with a view to strengthening this cooperative relationship, [between public and private recreation agencies], but so far, a solution satisfactory to all concerned, has not been found. Edmonton however, is not unique in this respect — many cities across the country being faced with similar problems which differ, largely, only in degree. Rather let it be considered a symptom of growth. With continued study during the coming year, I have little doubt that combined efforts to find the answer will ultimately prove successful.

> In the meantime, arrangements have been made for representatives of this Division to attend all meetings of the Recreation Commission in order that we may more fully understand the policies and the problems of that body, and be in a position to make contributions or representations whenever such seem desirable.

It is interesting to note that the large recreation survey was also an early example of the effect of different personalities on the work of the Council. Lillian Thomson, coming from a social work background, was very much interested in the development of social agencies and particularly in promoting the case work method as an approach to social work. When Hazeldine Bishop was hired as Executive Director in June of 1944, she brought with her a greater emphasis on research and planning as well as an interest in widening the base and scope of the Council.

One of Miss Bishop's first tasks for the Council was to evaluate its organization and operation. Her report, brought to the Executive Committee in October, 1944, made several recommendations. Her first observation was that the Council operated more like a "community council than like a Council of Social Agencies:

> Considering its structure, and its concern with matters relating to the social well-being of the community as a whole, with little regard for financial status, it appears that the Edmonton Council

of Social Agencies is, in reality, a community council. Moreover, if one looks at the local set-up, it becomes fairly obvious that only a community council could be expected to succeed here by reason of the fact that a very considerable number of the social welfare services which are available are sponsored, if not actually operated, by organizations which are not health or social welfare agencies and which were established primarily for some other and quite different purpose. Therefore, to acquire any coordination of existing services and plans for the best utilization of Edmonton's resources, these organizations must form part of the Council.

Her recommendations included the suggestion that the Council and the Federation of Community Leagues work closely together and that the name of the Council be changed to one "more descriptive of its objectives, and which would avoid the implication of exclusive preoccupation with the affairs of 'social agencies' as they are popularly understood — i.e. as having a 'relief' or 'underprivileged' connotation." The name change was tabled for the time being, but the association with the Community Leagues certainly grew. Indeed by 1949, the emphasis of the Council on the welfare of the whole community, not just the poor, was made explicit in the Annual Report:

> From this [the Council's Objectives] it will be seen that any matter relating to the social welfare of *the community* (not just the economically or socially disadvantaged portion of the community), which member organizations of the Council feel deserves study and consideration in an effort to promote, cooperatively, better welfare services for Edmonton — is a job for the Council. The Council also, is an instrument for developing informed public opinion on social problems and, through it may be organized concerted, joint action in connection with changes and improvements in community welfare services.

This emphasis on the whole community can be seen through a short listing of some of the 'smaller' projects of the Council during the second half of the Forties. These include an endorsement of a federal housing program, a conference on facilities for teen-age girls, two leadership training sessions per year, a brief regarding playgrounds, a review of the province's Juvenile Offenders Act, the preparation of minimum standards for camps, study of the need for education for family life, and a survey of ethnic groups in order to provide more accessible aid to immigrants.

In addition to these smaller projects, the Council was also deeply involved in the formation of two new organizations. The first was an Emergency Housekeeper Service, designed to supply housekeepers to seniors to enable them to stay in their homes, or to families where this was necessary to keep the family together and in the home in situations of health, or other, emergency. This organization was, at first, operated by the Junior Hospital League and later, became a part of the Family Service Bureau.

The other important agency which the Council helped to form was the John Howard Society. Dr. Douglas Smith, president of the Council in 1954, was very much involved in the formation of this organization. In high school, Smith had been interested in military affairs and involved in the high school cadet corps. Thus, when he began work as Lecturer in psychology at the University of Alberta in 1937, he also became involved with the Canadian Officer Training Corps and the Militia at the university. This led to a posting, first, as Personnel Officer, and then, as Staff Officer in the Regular Army. These activities led to his interest in social work:

> "For four years I was in Defence Headquarters. I saw all of the workings, saw the social workers in action, and saw the importance of that work. The personnel field and social work were quite related. The social workers were new in the Army. Their job was to help stem the wastage.
>
> . . . There had been the Archambault Report that pointed to the evils in the Penitentiary system, a very idealistic report. Then, after the war, a friend of mine from the Navy conducted a second report. It was more realistic, pointed out some of the things that could be done. It was that interest in solving the wastage and in the penal system that lead me into involvement with the John Howard Society and the Council. They were all very related in my mind." (Interview, Dr. D. E. Smith, March 5, 1990)

The work of the Council in relation to the development of the John Howard Society is a good example of much of the work that has been done over the years by the Council. In this case, there was a community concern over the problems of rehabilitation of ex-prisoners.

The Council called a public meeting in September, 1947. The meeting included,

> ... the Mayor and Chief of Police of Edmonton, several from the RCMP, the university, the legal profession, various churches, social agencies, the Canadian Legion, and the Councils of Social Agencies of Calgary and Lethbridge. A committee was appointed and the Council of Social Agencies was commissioned to secure further information and prepare a plan for consideration at a future meeting. (Special Report on the John Howard Society, October 1950).

Hazeldine Bishop, Executive Director of the Council, provided the professional backup for the work of the committee. It took less than a year for this committee to do its work. Miss Bishop reported to a Council Executive Committee meeting on June 3, 1948 that a John Howard Society had been officially organized on April 28 of that year and expected to be in operation with an executive secretary/caseworker by mid August. Thus, in this case, the organizational committee was not a committee of the Council's as had been the case with In-city camps or the medical social worker, but was instead a committee of the community which relied on the Council of Social Agencies for support. The Executive Director's report to the 1948 Annual Meeting described this kind of Council activity:

> One natural outcome of continuous study of the policies and pro-grammes of existing social services, is the recognition of unmet needs, or gaps in community services. In consequence, the Council is frequently in a position to be of considerable assistance to citizens' groups which are contemplating the initiation of some new social welfare venture, either by suggesting to them, when consulted, unfilled areas of service which they might fill, or, in helping them to assess the value of the new service which they are thinking of starting.

> If satisfied that the new service is needed, in the interests of the welfare of the City, the Council may go further and place at the disposal of the sponsoring group, such resources as it has, in the nature of secretarial assistance, technical information, and advice — until such time as the new organization has become well established and in a position to carry on alone.

> During the past year the Council staff rendered assistance of this

kind to two new social service organizations — namely, the John Howard Society of Alberta, and the still newer recreational club for elderly people — which only last week had its first club gathering at the Recreation Building and was officially named by its members — 'The Edmonton Friendship Club'. Your Director serves as an Advisory member on the boards of both of these organizations; and also continues to act in like capacity on the Junior Hospital League Committee, operating the Emergency Housekeeper Service, which was launched in a similar way — with the help of the Council — two years ago.

Giving this kind of professional support to fledgling services has been a staple of the Council's work and in so doing, the Council has had a hand in the development of a remarkably large part of the social welfare network in Edmonton.

Despite all of this activity, however, the area that took the largest amount of staff and volunteer time and was most hotly discussed in the second half of the forties was the matter of child welfare. In Miss Bishop's 1944 evaluation report she had recommended that "separation of child care and family agencies is an artificial and impractical arrangement leading to duplication of effort, and that one Child and Family Division of the Council be formed including all agencies having primary interest in this field. This recommendation, adopted at the 1944 Annual Meeting, was important since the next several years in Alberta social welfare history were to be marked by tumultuous events in the child welfare field.

Chapter Four

Like a Missionary Venture

From the time of Marjorie Bradford's 1929 survey of social welfare in Alberta, it had been noted that the child welfare field was lacking in both expertise and appropriate facilities. The Children's Aid Society in Edmonton operated one home for children, but carried on no other children's aid functions. Children who were neglected or delinquent were housed in several large children's institutions or in foster homes of uncertain quality. Early in 1943, the Child Welfare Division of the Council began its first foray into the study of this area. For the meeting of February 24, 1943, the program committee suggested Juvenile Delinquency, Adoptions, Child Placement, Children's Institutions, and Day Nursery Care as five possible subjects for study. They had, however, hardly begun their work when, in June, the Executive Committee of the Council took over the job, having been requested to prepare a report for the Provincial Committee on Child Welfare. In the Introduction to the report, delivered to the government in August, the Council outlined their intent:

In this report we plan:

(a) to outline some of the procedures now accepted as standard child welfare practice by national organizations like the Canadian Welfare Council and the Child Welfare League of America as well as by hundreds of provincial, state and local agencies over this Continent.

(b) in light of these standard practices to discuss some aspects of present child welfare services in our own Province.

(c) to make suggestions and recommendations which, we sincerely hope, will be immediately helpful to your Committee and through the Committee to all children in need of official care.

In Section One, the report described the nature of case work. It pointed out the necessity for a social case study for each case, "observation coupled with a knowledge of psychology," and consultation with other professionals such as doctors, nurses, clergy, school teachers, and other social service workers. It made a special point that consulting the Council's Social Service Exchange was an important part of the professional case work process.

After describing the standard procedure, and noting that the provincial Child Welfare Branch did not make use of the Social Service Exchange, the report went on to make very plain what the Council thought of the province's practice, particularly in making children wards of the government:

> The statistics of the Child Welfare and Mothers' Allowance Branch show the causes of neglect among children who were made government wards and presumably separated from their own parents. In 59% of the 543 cases in 1942 the cause of neglect is stated as 'mother unable to support'. This reason was also given for 67% of the 297 cases in 1941. These figures suggest practices so far out of alignment with standard procedures that we feel there must be some other explanation of the action taken. Nevertheless the fact remains that even the use of the terminology in question indicates some divergence from an accepted standard, namely that no child is removed from his parents for financial reasons only.
>
> If standard procedures are to be followed as suggested throughout this report, qualified personnel is indispensable .... The widespread acceptance of such opinions is exemplified by the fact that since the first Great War some half dozen Canadian Schools of Social Work have been opened to meet a growing demand for qualified personnel, a demand which comes not by any means from voluntary agencies only, but from the Dominion Government, the Armed Forces, and from some Provincial and Municipal Governments. We do not know of any child welfare or probation officer in this province who is a graduate of a School of Social Work or has had comparable preliminary training in the social sciences.

The Council Report made nineteen recommendations for improvement of the province's child welfare procedures, but the most crucial came at the end:

> Anyone who has taken a thoughtful interest in Alberta's child

welfare services must be well aware that the present program has developed over a long period of time. Complete overnight change cannot be reasonably expected. Yet procrastination is to be avoided. At the earliest possible date the foundation of a new child welfare program should be firmly laid. How can this be done? . . .

We recommend:

(1) That arrangements be made for an official survey of child welfare services in this Province.
(2) That as a first choice the Canadian Welfare Council be asked to conduct this Survey because of its long experience in such service to Canadian communities.
(3) That the Child Welfare League of America be considered, if necessary, as a second choice. The League is also well equipped for survey work and since it has no possible connection with any Alberta group might be deemed more impartial than a Canadian organization.

In fact, the province did not take up this recommendation of a study and instead passed a revised and consolidated Child Welfare Act in 1944. The rumours of inadequate child care continued. By October of 1945, the Executive Committee of the Council asked the now enlarged Child and Family Division to "undertake a study of child welfare services in Edmonton, including maintenance and custodial care and services for juvenile delinquents".(Minutes, Child and Family Division, October 25, 1945) After discussion, the Division decided this was too broad a study for them to undertake, but agreed to begin a smaller study of existing services for the care and treatment of juvenile delinquents.

Thus, the scene was set for the Whitton study into welfare in Alberta sponsored by the Imperial Order of the Daughters of the Empire (IODE). The Edmonton Chapter of the IODE, one of the initial members of the Council of Social Agencies, was not happy with the state of child welfare in Alberta. The Council of Social Agencies did not have the resources to proceed with an overall survey. Whether the IODE consulted the Council specifically at this point is not certain. However, they did take up the Council's recommendation and hire Dr. Charlotte Whitton from the Canadian Welfare Council to do a complete survey of welfare practices. The picture which emerged was not positive. E. Stewart Bishop describes coming to do social work in Alberta at the time as,

". . . like a missionary venture. My parents had come to Alberta in 1905 as missionaries in the Methodist Church. So, for me, the idea of what was happening [in Alberta] after the war particularly around this scandal compared to the sophistication of the child welfare system in Ontario was horrifying." (Interview, E. Stewart Bishop, March 7, 1990)

The scandal to which Mr. Bishop refers was the adoption scandal uncovered by Charlotte Whitton:

"[The adoption practices] were pretty weird I can assure you. The Superintendent of Welfare was a chap who had come from England. He was a one man show. He was reported to have bundled kids in his car and driven out on the highway and stopped off at farms and said 'How'd you like a baby?' And I have no reason to believe that wasn't pretty close to the mark. He also arranged international adoptions which were pretty badly frowned on because how can you check them out . . . .

The first time I met him I went down to his office. Hazeldine [Bishop] had said 'just look at his walls'. They were absolutely plastered with pictures of all these babies. He knew them all personally. He'd actually placed them personally. And I think it's safe to say that despite the fact that the program was whitewashed, it was substandard to what was going on elsewhere in the rest of Canada.

But in order to try to get things started, the IODE had engaged Charlotte Whitton to do this study. Now Charlotte Whitton was an extremely contentious person. She was a sort of 'Madame Welfare', certainly the most prominent person in welfare at that time, though I would say notorious is a better word. She was not a professional social worker.

The study was delayed a number of years because she had other assignments that took her away. But eventually she came out and she really flailed the government. And at one point, people who have studied this episode really closely said it became very clear suddenly the government shut her off and were not going to co-operate any more.

This didn't deter Charlotte. She wrote an article in the *New Liberty* magazine that was published in Toronto. It was a kind of editorial-feature article about adoptions in Alberta. Well, within a week, the offices of the *New Liberty* magazine were raided by the RCMP and charges of conspiracy to commit liable were laid against Charlotte and the editor, and Charlotte was demanding that she go to jail. Someone got her out on $25,000 bail and she made hay out of this. This was her forte. She made it so damn hot for the government, it became a nationwide scandal.

The way they got out of it was they dropped the charges in favour of setting up a Royal Commission. They appointed a Judge Howson to do it . . . . The net result was to put a freeze on the provincial government being involved with social workers at all, period, because it embarrassed the government and the civil service. Dr. Cross and the whole bunch of them would have nothing to do with social workers for many years." (Stewart Bishop, March 7, 1990)

Certainly, Whitton and the colleagues who assisted her did not mince words in the report. The Home Investigating Committee of the Provincial Child Welfare Commission was described as operating "a mail order service' comparable to practice outmoded and condemned for over a generation by responsible child welfare services, public or private." (*Welfare in Alberta*, 1947) The practice of placing boys and girls in "free" foster homes where the children were intended to work in return for their care instead of in foster homes subsidized by the province was criticized as child labour. The practice of sending babies off to many parts of the United States for adoption with no more investigation than mailed references was even more roundly condemned. "Few people would buy even registered stock or pets upon such a basis." Whitton's description in the preface of the powers of the Superintendent of Child Welfare leaves no doubt as to her opinion of the Alberta system:

The Superintendent of Child Welfare, directly or through the Commission, holds and exercises powers without parallel in any enactment in the Study's knowledge except one in Hitler's Germany and certain provisions in the code of the Soviet Union . . . .

This was the first major occasion in its history when the Council found itself in the position of having to decide when and how to criticize an organization with which it needed to co-operate. It was a difficult position. Although neither the Council nor its staff were involved in actually writing the *Welfare in Alberta* report, the close links between Charlotte Whitton, the Canadian Welfare Council, and the Council of Social Agencies were well known. Indeed, the office used by Whitton and the other report writers was only one floor above the Council's office in the Tegler Building, and the association of the Council with the Report was clear in the public mind.

The Council acted with great care. At an Executive Committee meeting in December 1946, Mr. S.W. Field, then President of the Council, reported on his meeting with Dr. Cross, the Minister of Health and Public Welfare; Mr. C.B. Hill, the Superintendent of Child Welfare, and other provincial officials:

> The interview had revealed considerable misunderstanding regarding the functions of the Council and the work which it was attempting to do, and it had been finally agreed that the Departments under Dr. Cross's jurisdiction would remain within the membership of the Council for another six months, with a view to determining whether or not it was possible for satisfactory working relationships to be developed. Dr. Cross had agreed to appoint official delegates to the Council, and correspondence between Mr. Field and Dr. Cross on this point was read. It had been further agreed that the Council Executive would appoint a liaison committee to meet with Departmental officials from time to time on matters of mutual interest. The Department had further been promised that the Council would not publicly criticize it without clearing with Dr. Cross first.(Minutes, Dec. 12, 1946)

In fact, before Dr. Cross could appoint any official delegates to the Council, the charges and counter-charges reported in the newspapers had created so much ill-feeling that no delegates were ever appointed.

By August, 1947, the Royal Commission Investigation of the Provincial Child Welfare Department had been set up, and the Council called a special meeting of its member organizations to discuss preparing a brief; forty-four people attended. It was agreed that the Council would submit a brief to the Commission on behalf of its member organizations but that the individual organization who wished to might also present their own briefs. The Council prepared its brief and presented it to another special meeting in November. In keeping with its attempts to remain in a position to co-operate with the Child Welfare Branch, the Council 'was not making specific charges but instead was taking a positive approach making recommendations followed by discussion of reasons for these recommendations and by illustrative case material . . .' (Minutes, November 24, 1947) The Council's brief included forty-four specific recommendations on all aspects of child welfare.

The Royal Commission's findings were stated in less alarming language than those of the IODE's report. Nevertheless, it did make over twenty recommendations, which supported Whitton's main charges. In particular, the Commission recommended,

— That the Child Welfare Branch recognize what is known as family case work as a sound procedure, tending to keep children in their own families, and take whatever steps may be required to make this service generally available throughout the province.
— That steps be taken in recognition of the partnership of the Child Welfare Branch with, and dependence upon, private agencies in the care and custody of children, so that a full measure of co-operation, assistance, leadership, and guidance will be furnished to these agencies.
— That intensive and systematic search be made for foster homes for non-adoptable children, and . . . in the interests of the child, more and more for paid foster homes, and a curtailment of 'work' homes . . .
— That cross-border placements of children should be discontinued.(Report of the Royal Commission, 1947)

That the lengthy Royal Commission report supported almost all of Dr. Whitton's findings,

. . . was not at all what the government had expected and was definitely not to its liking. The Minister of Health and Welfare moved immediately with an order to the Commission's Secretariat that absolutely no copies of the original document should be made . . . . To the Commission's Secretariat the 'no copies' order was a clear signal of the government's intent and some concerned staff members leaked the information to an Edmonton group of Dr. Whitton's supporters. Among them was Hazeldine Bishop . . . . With her assistance, including the use of the Council's office, several volunteer typists, plus extra typewriters, were organized for an all-night session. At the secretariat's closing time, the day before the Minister's presentation [to the legislature], the 'sacred' master copy was smuggled out and the typists set to work to transcribe every page onto a Gestetner stencil. (No copy machines in those days.) And by seven o'clock the next morning the job was done and the original safely returned. Subsequently, at a more leisured pace, some three hundred copies were run off — about the maximum for such stencils. (Anguish, "Decades of Disgrace", unpublished mss.)

The day after the all night typing job, Minister Cross dismissed the Royal Commission in the legislature as a report done by judges who knew little of child welfare. As far as the provincial government's child welfare department was concerned, that was the end of the story.

As for the province embracing professional social workers, case work, and co-operation with the private organizations, there was little progress for several years until personnel had changed at both the Ministerial and Deputy Ministerial level. Jack Anguish, Executive Director of the Council from 1951 to 1954, describes the effect of this scandal on subsequent work of the Council with the government:

"As a matter of fact I think I spent a lot of my time trying to develop a liaison with, at least, the staff level of the Health and Welfare Ministry; it was Health and Welfare at one time and then split. When they split, they brought in a really fine man as Minister, by the name of Halmrast. He was a sheep rancher. It wasn't long after he was there, I got a call from him and he asked if I would come down and see him.

I went down, sort of quaking, because any approach we had to the previous Minister, he would just turn his back and gaze out the window while you talked. So I didn't know what to expect. He closed his door, told his secretary to hold his calls, shut off his intercom, and then said, 'I understand that our child welfare program leaves something to be desired. Tell me about it.' I said, 'Are you serious sir?' And I spent an hour talking with him . . . . Things started to move. Then the Minister of Agriculture was killed in an accident, and Halmrast was moved to Agriculture . . . . From there on, we just retrogressed again." (Interview, Jack Anguish, March 26, 1990)

While progress was slow provincially, the publicity had a different effect on the city. During the Royal Commission Hearings, it became clear that the City's Civic Relief Department staff were very closely connected to the provincial staff. City Council consulted with

Hazeldine Bishop about what could be done to bring the Civic Relief and Children's Aid Department up to par. Miss Bishop's response was to suggest the hiring of a qualified professional social worker to head the city's department. Thus, at the City's request, she negotiated with E. Stewart Bishop (no relation), and he was hired in September, 1949 as Superintendent for the Civic Relief and Children's Aid Department. By the time of the Council's 1949 Annual Meeting, "Most harmonious relationships between the [City] Department and the Council [had] already been established, . . . (Annual Report, 1949). This connection between the City Department, Stewart Bishop, and the Council would have far reaching effects on the Council's future.

Summary

1939 - 1949:
The Pioneer Years — Summary

The first ten years of the Edmonton Council of Social Agencies were years of intense activity in the social welfare field, in both the public and private sectors. The effect of both the Depression and World War II had been to cause the federal government in particular to take more responsibility for social welfare, and particularly to take over more and more of the income security aspects of welfare. The Edmonton Council, formed somewhat later than similar councils in eastern Canada, took an active part in the discussions of the changing views of public and private responsibility, noting in its first Annual Report that there was, in Canada, an increasing acceptance of personal responsibility for the common good.

The Council provided, for Edmonton, the first central focus of activity for the private, voluntary sector. Through its four Divisions, it identified issues of concern and gaps in the service network; it organized groups to study the needs and develop new services; it provided professional support to new agencies as they began their work. When Hazeldine Bishop took over the Executive Director's position in 1944, the Council began to add research studies to these other major services, as well as to broaden its base from social agencies to community agencies in general.

In addition, to its central role within the voluntary sector, the Council worked to promote the use of professional case work methods in all social work and to enhance the recognition of social work as a profession. It was one of several organizations which was involved in identifying major problems in the child welfare services of Alberta, an issue that was to dominate the social policy landscape in the 1950s.

Section Two

1950 – 59:
Transition and Growth

Chapter Five

Upset, Transition, and Change

As the Council of Social Agencies moved into the 1950s, there was uneasiness and dissatisfaction. The initial enthusiasm of social agencies for the work of the Council seemed to have waned. Use of the Social Service Exchange was falling off. The Community Chest found itself competing with many other charitable appeals. Some sectors of the community, dismayed by the child welfare controversy and its criticism of government, no longer supported the Council's work in the way they had. Attendance at Division meetings was not as high, thus causing more work to fall on the shoulders of the Executive Director.

In April, 1950, Robert Chapman, a member of the Council's Executive Committee and local business man, raised the issue at an Executive Committee meeting:

> Mr. Chapman described a number of incidents which had come to his attention recently, indicating that the work which the Council was doing, and its value in the total community welfare picture, was not generally understood. This observation appeared to be true, not only of the public generally, but also of a great many members of the Community Chest Budget Committee and Board of Directors, and even of the boards of some of the member organizations. This being so, Mr. Chapman proposed that a strong public relations and publicity committee should be appointed to conduct an intensive interpretation programme, starting immediately. He further proposed that the Management Committee of the Executive be charged with responsibility for giving detailed consideration to ways and means to developing such a programme, also that it be requested to study Council objectives, immediate and long term. (Minutes, Executive Committee, April 12, 1950)

Thus began the first, though certainly not the last, period of internal examination and discussion through which Council members over the years have struggled to describe and define the work of this organization which has proven so often not to be easily defined.

The Management Committee met the following week and outlined an extensive public relations plan which included meeting individually with the Community Chest's Directors and Budget Committee members, attending Board meetings of other member agencies to describe the Council's work, and launching a publicity campaign for the general public. It was further decided that the Executive Committee itself should devote a meeting to a full discussion of the Council and its work before any publicity campaign was launched. Finally, the April 19 meeting recommended that the Council's name be changed:

> The name of the Council was again the subject of discussion, it being felt that it does not adequately reflect the aims of the Council, and that for this reason, it is a distinct and unnecessary handicap to the Council in gaining general understanding of its purposes.

The name was subsequently changed to the Edmonton Council of Community Services, and the Executive Committee proceeded with some public relations work. Nevertheless, by the time of the 1951 budget meeting, matters had not improved:

> The matter [Council-Chest relations] was raised at this point because of its relation to the 1951 budget. Mr. Chapman reported that criticism of the Council in the Chest Board, of which we have been aware for some time, was openly voiced at the recent Chest Board meeting at which our budget had finally been approved, after considerable discussion. The Chest Board had requested that a delegation from the Council meet with them to try to resolve these differences by clarifying the value of the Council's work.

The Council, through the forties, had done several studies at the request of the Chest, including studies of the Alberta Humane Society, the Home for Ex-Servicemen's Children, the Edmonton Creche and Day Nursery, the John Howard Society, and the Emergency Housekeeper Service. Nevertheless, the core of the criticism from the Chest was that the Council was an expensive agency (now with an additional staff hired to assist the Executive Director) whose work did not seem all that tangible when compared to a summer camp, for instance, and which sometimes stirred up trouble with agencies and donors. The Council accepted the Chest's invitation to meet, and armed with a three page list of the Council's tangible accomplishments, a delegation of eight met with the Chest's Directors in March:

> The President . . . felt that they had been well received, and that the information regarding the Council's work which had been presented to the meeting, had been very helpful, particularly in clarifying the role of the Council and its justification for continued Chest support. He was of the opinion that misunderstanding and difficulties between the Chest and Council would be very much less likely to arise in the future . . . . It was further noted that at this meeting, there were some who were still under the impression that the total cost of central services was disproportionately high - the Family Service Bureau having been mistakenly viewed as a central service - and that it had been agreed that a committee comprising the presidents of the Community Chest, Council of Community Services, Family Service Bureau, and the chairman of the Budget Committee should meet and explore the possibilities of effecting savings through amalgamation or closer coordination among these three organizations. (Minutes, Executive Committee, April 9, 1951).

For the next few months, relations between Chest and Council did improve somewhat. Discussions began about the possibility of amalgamating the two organizations. Hazeldine Bishop, however, was not in favour of this. She had served as the Executive Secretary of the Chest from 1945 to 1947, and had felt then that the research and planning work of the Council suffered when the staff was also doing the work of the Chest. However, in August, 1951, Miss Bishop tendered her resignation. She had been offered, and had accepted, a position with the London, Ontario Council of Community Services.

This left the Council Executive with a problem. The early fifties were a seller's market for social work graduates. The social service field was expanding rapidly and graduates could have their pick of jobs. By October, the Personnel Committee had only two applications, neither of which seemed satisfactory. Dr. Douglas Smith, chair of the Personnel Committee, recommended that Hazeldine Bishop's assistant, Mr. A.C. Ashby be appointed Acting Director from October 15, 1951 to March 31, 1952. Then, the Personnel Committee went on an active search for applicants. Jack Anguish, who was ultimately hired describes that search from his perspective:

"I was Associate Secretary of what they called the Chests and Councils Division of the Canadian Welfare Council in Ottawa. I had heard that Edmonton was looking for a Council Director, so I came in early one day, pulled my typewriter over, and started a letter to Dr. Douglas Smith, because I'd heard that he was the search man. I'd just finished typing 'Dear Dr. Smith' when the phone rang and it was Dr. Smith. I literally dropped the phone and almost blew his ear off. He wanted to know if I knew of anybody who would be interested in the job, so I said, 'Yeah, me'. So we had quite a long chat, and then a couple of weeks later the President of the time, Dorothy Love, was down to Ottawa. She came in and I spent a whole day being quizzed on everything including 'Was I interested in football?' Then she stopped and said, 'Oh my word'. That was the last year that Ottawa had won the Grey Cup. Anyhow that signed, sealed, and delivered it [the job]." (Interview, Jack Anguish, March 26, 1990)

On March 24, the Executive appointed Jack Anguish as Executive Director at a salary of $5500 per year. Mr. Ashby, who had applied for the Director's job himself, indicated that his resignation would be effective from March 31. Thus for April, and most of May until Anguish arrived, the Council was without any Executive staff. In addition, the long time secretary, Mrs. Fisher, had suffered an accident during the winter, and so the office was staffed with a series of temporary appointments. With the Executive Committee being split from their deliberations on the choice of Executive Director, the Council was in a state of disarray when Mr. Anguish arrived:

"To begin with I found that I had walked into an Executive Committee that was split right down the middle as to whether the other assistant should have been hired or I should have been hired. I had quite a difficult time there for a month or two and then it all sort of straightened around." (Anguish, March 26, 1990)

There were other problems as well. Relations with the Chest were still difficult, and the work of the Divisions simply hadn't picked up. Community interest seemed to be at an all time low. In January of 1953, the new Director presented the Executive Committee with a special brief, prepared on his own initiative, outlining what he saw to be the central problems. In this report, Anguish outlined the two models of Council operation which he saw as typical, then came down firmly on the side of the second, more "democratic" model:

One [approach] might be described as organizing the council so that it operates, in effect, as another social agency, of and by itself, providing central services such as research, consultation, advice, dissemination of information, etc. to its members and the community. This type of council tends to operate as a series of 'brain trusts' and derives its strengths from hand picked committee personnel and the status of these individuals in the community. It functions more as a planning board than as a council in the true sense of the word. It tends to plan for the community rather than with it . . . .

The other type of organization depends more on its member agencies and the persons delegated by them to do its work. In addition to delegates such a council usually draws in a number of individual members who are interested in and concerned about the social welfare of the community, but these members are distinctly subordinate to organizations. This type of council is essentially a council of community organizations, and works through and on behalf of these organizations. At least in the early stages it would deal mainly with problems brought to it by its members and would carry on its work through project committees formed from organizational representatives and individuals genuinely interested in the particular problem.

The main strength of this type of council lies in the development of broad participation and support throughout the community. Like all democratic action this may take longer, but if real participation is developed genuine support and lasting action usually follow. (Special Report by the Executive Director to the Executive Committee, January 7, 1953)

With this report, then, Anguish prompted a major reworking of the Council's approach and structure. The Executive Committee opted for the democratic model, attempting to draw in as broad a range of participants from the community organizations as possible. The Division structure was abandoned as one which created artificial separations between agencies and topics. Instead of being a separate professional social work voice, the Council would now be more of a voice of its member agencies. Henceforth, when an issue was brought to the Council by one of its agencies, a project committee would be formed to study it, and recommendations made to a Board of Directors who would make the policy decisions.

This plan was presented to a general meeting of all the member agencies and agreed to. A committee was formed to draft necessary changes to the By-laws, and work went ahead. This was not, however, all of the structural change that was to take place. At the same time as these discussions were taking place, the Community Chest was still pursuing the subject of amalgamation of the two organizations. But with the change of Executive Director had come a definite change in point of view on combined Chests and Councils.

Jack Anguish had been Director of a combined Chest and Council in Brantford, Ontario; then he was Director of a Community Chest in Windsor and developed a Council as part of it, before he had moved to the Chests and Councils Division of the Canadian Welfare Council. Thus he had a good deal of experience with the combination of Chest and Council and felt that it was a workable arrangement. The negotiations were carried out and in February 1953, Anguish was appointed the Executive Secretary of the Council and the Chest at a salary of $6000. He hired Angus Brunlees to be the Campaign Chairman for the Chest and by December of 1953 it was agreed by both the Chest and the Council that an assistant for the Council must be hired as well. Anguish hired Bill Nicholls for that position. Each organization kept its own Board of Directors, but from 1953 to 1960, they operated with joint staff. Jack Anguish found it a positive arrangement:

"I thought it [the combined Chest and Council] worked very well. It was sort of a cross-pollination process. I was able to bring to the attention of the big shots on the Chest Board a lot of the community issues that they hadn't even thought about. And we did work together pretty well on that score. For instance, Vic Macosham of Macosham Van Lines was on the [Chest] Board, . . . Vic was funny. The first time I met with the Chest when I was taking over, I was sitting down at the far end of the Board table, and he was way up at the top, and I can still hear him, peering down at me, saying 'So that's your goddamn social worker from the East'. It was a relationship I'll always cherish. It worked out pretty well. Of course, a lot depended on how you could staff it. Bill Nicholls was a big help to me." (Anguish, March 26, 1990)

Thus, as the Annual Report of 1953 stated, 'For the third consecutive year it is necessary for the President to preface his report with the comment the past year, for the Council, has been one of upset and change'. This period of change was coming to an end, however. With the first year of the combined Chest and Council behind them, the staff were much more able to cope with all the demands. In fact, a period of stability, productivity, and growth was beginning.

Chapter Six

Liaison Work

The approach to Council work during the fifties could be summed up, according to Jack Anguish, as liaison work, "trying to pull together the various organizations and factions that were working on a specific problem, rather than going hell bent for election on their own route, and I think we were reasonably successful in that way" (Anguish, March 26, 1990) Indeed, looking at the range of work which the Council initiated or participated in during the decade indicates considerable success.

The fifties was a time of expansion in Alberta. Mining was doing well; the north was increasingly an area of economic growth. Oil had been discovered and was providing the basis for an economic boom, although it wasn't universally welcomed:

> "It took me a year and a half before I could convince anybody on the Chest Board that we should have someone from the oil business on the Board because they resented it. I've heard them say 'One of the worst things that ever happened to Edmonton was the discovery of oil'. It upset the whole comfortable centre of supply for the north. People were streaming in, new businesses were popping up." (Anguish, March 26, 1990)

In such an environment, it was not surprising that there was a concomitant increase in both social problems and community organizations which attempted to solve them.

One of the first problems that came to the Council in the fifties was the problems of transients. At a Child and Family Division meeting in February, 1950, the issue was raised. Representatives from the National Employment Service, the John Howard Association, the YMCA, the Canadian Legion, and the Ministerial Association all spoke up as to the growing problem. Men who had worked in the mines or the oil fields were laid off in the winters and streamed to Edmonton, with money in their pockets for the first few days, but after that with very little. Others, some with families, were travelling from across the country looking for work. The suggestion was raised that a central clothing and temporary assistance depot be set up, but this was not met with approval:

> In general discussion, it was seriously questioned whether it would be wise to centralize this work, lest it prove a magnet and accentuate the problem still further. . . . It was felt that the care of transients was clearly a national problem, but the possibilities of finding any immediate solution at that level was recognised as remote. Under existing conditions, it was felt any alleviation of the situation would have to come through Provincial, Municipal, and private effort. Most municipalities make some provision for shelter of homeless men and transients. Edmonton, however, has not done so , since the Province has legal responsibility for the transient and non-resident. The accommodation provided by the Province, however, at the Old Immigration Hall, appears totally inadequate to meet the present need, being occupied to a large extent by permanent residents who are unemployable and charges upon the Department of Public Welfare, or who are Old Age Pensioners. (Minutes, Child and Family Division, February 21, 1950)

The conclusion of this meeting was that further study was needed, and such further study was undertaken right through the decade. Several attempts were made at improving the situation. A Committee on Services to Transients was formed and in 1952 an attempt was made to survey the dimensions of the problem:

> A form for reporting applications for assistance had been devised and sent out to all major organization known to be giving services including over 100 churches . . . . So far only 11 organizations have reported but these have reported 179 different individuals in the period July 21st to Aug. 3rd. Most of the major organizations are reporting but unfortunately so far nothing has been received from either the Provincial Single Men's Division Hostel or from Hope Mission.(Minutes, Executive Committee, Sept. 5, 1952)

The co-operation from the Provincial Department did not improve quickly. In 1954, the Committee sent a delegation to the Minister:

> "When our small delegation arrived we were greeted courteously

by the new Minister, but Mr. Miller [Deputy Minister], sitting beside his desk, merely nodded without even standing up. Our spokesman was Dean Sparling of the Anglican cathedral. During his presentation the Minister, I am still convinced, listened both politely and thoughtfully. Mr. Miller, on the other hand, simply scowled and stared into space somewhere over my head.

'Well, gentlemen,' the Minister said at the end, 'it does seem to me that you have a real problem.' Then, turning to his deputy, 'Is there not something we can do to help, Mr. Miller?'

'No!' Mr. Miller snapped — the only word he uttered during the entire session.

Appearing somewhat nonplussed, the Minister turned back to the Dean. 'I am sorry, gentlemen, but I'm afraid there is nothing we can do.'

And with that he stood up and politely ushered us out, leaving Mr. Miller still sitting and scowling." (Anguish, p. 41)

The Committee on Services to Transients felt that a central registry would be essential to co-ordinate services, determine who got sent to which available beds, and otherwise ensure that resources were used as carefully as possible, but although there were several attempts, such a registry was not established. Instead, the Provincial Department of Public Welfare did accept the responsibility for transients, and developed its own registration system for the Hostel. It also opened an additional facility for 170 at the Municipal Airport. Nevertheless, the city's facilities were still overtaxed. In 1957, a letter went from the Chief of Police to Stewart Bishop, by then a Vice-President of the Council as well as head of the City Welfare Department, noting that 84 transients had been housed in the cell block in the first 23 days of November because they had nowhere else to go.

In 1959, the Committee on Transients met, with 12 organizations represented, and reviewed the situation once again. They identified problems including difficulty with co-ordination of services, lack of money or accommodation for men awaiting a first paycheque, and lack of money for transportation to jobs outside of Edmonton. In addition, Stewart Bishop raised the question of whether "our very philosophy of quick material assistance and keeping-them-moving to other centres, create[s] the 'professional hobo' type?" (Memorandum to Board of Directors, October 1959). With such questions in mind, the Committee did not set another meeting date, but agreed to meet again, at some future time. The problem of transients was to continue as an important Council concern into the 1960s and '70s.

Another issue of concern which surfaced in 1950 and continued through the decade was the matter of services to people with disabilities. The Health Division of the Council had been inactive in the late forties, partly because some of its strongest leadership had left. However, as the 1950s began, there was considerable increase in the problems of persons with various health disabilities, particularly crippled children. Dr. Herbert Meltzer, an outstanding surgeon, and Medical Director of the Charles Camsell Hospital, had joined the Board of the Council, and took on the leadership of a revived Health Division.

In June 1950, the Health Division met and began a fact-finding study about the various services available to crippled children and the numbers involved. One of the problems which presented itself was that the crippled children's organizations did their work with very specific groups of children, and some children who were crippled were left out. Thus, for example, the Edmonton Cerebral Palsy Association had formed only seven weeks before coming to the Health Division meeting largely because of a feeling that the cerebral palsied child was not served by other organizations. The Crippled Children's Fund reported that their fund was available to any child,

> . . . for whom their medical board felt that medical or surgical attention would be of assistance. The policy was very flexible, with no limitations being placed upon the amount of money which could be spent on any one case, or upon age, nationality, religion, etc. Only about 10 percent of the cases assisted to date, came from the city of Edmonton, and very few of these have been spastics. However, if such a case were judged by the medical board as likely to be benefited, it would be acceptable for assistance from the Fund. (Minutes, Health Division, June 1, 1950)

Clearly, there was some difference of opinion between these two groups as to the availability of the funds to children with cerebral palsy.

Along with these two organizations, there were several other groups working with crippled children, including the Junior Hospital League which had been working with polio cases at the University Hospital, the Red Cross, the Shrine Club, the Canadian Rheumatism and Arthritis Society, and a Provincial Government programme for polio victims. Some type of co-ordination seemed necessary. An added incentive for co-ordinating was the fact that the Canadian Council for Crippled Children, which undertook the Easter Seal Campaign each year, had no branch in Alberta, but was considering going national with its fund-raising campaign. If there were no local branch, the existing groups worried that money collected for crippled children in Alberta would go to services in other provinces.

Thus, in early 1951, an Alberta Council for Crippled Children was formed and eighteen agencies that dealt with these children joined immediately. Co-ordination was not to be carried out that simply in this instance, however, because of the creation of a rival organization:

A major and somewhat disturbing complication had arisen with the incorporation on March 15th of an Alberta Society for Crippled Children. This Society, which was to be largely composed of parents, relatives, and friends of crippled children, had resulted from efforts made by the Edmonton Cerebral Palsy Association to organize a rival agency to the Council for Crippled Children. The primary motivation appeared to be competition for the franchise to sell Easter seals in Alberta in future, and prevention of the franchise passing to the coordinating body already established — namely, the Alberta Council for Crippled Children. Plans were being made by both organizations to have representation at the Winnipeg meeting of the Canadian Council for Crippled Children on May 11th at which the claims of each would be submitted and considered.(Minutes, Executive Council, April 9, 1951)

As well as competing for the Easter Seals franchise, it can be noted that these two organizations demonstrated different attitudes as to who was best able to represent the children's needs, the parents and friends, or the agencies. Be that as it may, the Canadian Council deferred its decision for 60 days and sent the rivals back to Edmonton to find a way to work together or to establish which was the strongest. Ultimately, the Alberta Council for Crippled Children did receive the Easter Seal franchise.

It was not too long, however, before it became apparent that there was a still larger constituency of rehabilitation service organizations and their clientele that was developing services and strategies for fund-raising. The local branch of the C.N.I.B. held a campaign of its own, during the same month as the Chest campaign, which upset the Board of the Community Chest considerably. Finally, a study group of all rehabilitation agencies was formed in 1953 under the Chairmanship of Mr. Leslie Gue, who had been appointed by the provincial government as Provincial Co-ordinator of Rehabilitation.

The Council was, at first, only one of the many agencies with representatives on the Study Group. However, by 1956, the Group had decided that their informal organization as a study group prevented them from taking any of the actions that now seemed essential. The Group approached the Council with a request to become affiliated with the Council, perhaps as a separate Division. The Council Board did agree to take on the job of co-ordinating the Study Group; it did not, however, feel that it had the necessary staff resources to set up an entire Division devoted to rehabilitation.

This committee of the Council's — it became the Standing Committee on Rehabilitation in 1958 — completed many studies, including a survey of services, a study of the voting rights of homebound or hospitalized people, a study of services for placement and employment, for vocational training for retarded children, and a study of the need and resources for prosthetic devices. Like the work with transients, the Standing Committee on Rehabilitation continued on into the sixties.

Two other projects of the fifties also illustrate the liaison work of the Council in that era. Already in the late forties, the Council had worked briefly with groups organized to work with immigrants and refugees. In 1949, they had carried out a survey of ethnic groups to identify sources of assistance for immigrants. But the inflow of immigrants from Europe throughout the fifties resulted in a similar growth in agencies to serve them. The Council again began the task of co-ordinating the work of these agencies, and continued to do so through the Hungarian Refugee crisis in 1956.

Similarly, the council brought together a number of interested individuals and groups around the question of mental health services. After considerable work and study, this committee recommended the starting of an Edmonton Mental Health Association in 1954. As in the situation of the crippled children's groups, there was a question of whether this group wished to affiliate with the national organization, the Canadian Mental Health Association. There were questions about the amount of local autonomy that a branch of the association would have compared to an independent local association. In addition, there was concern about fund raising since the Community Chest did not allow groups into membership whose national organizations conducted separate campaigns. The question was resolved in favour of joining the national body.

The Study on Aging, a major project of the Council's, began in a rather different way than these projects, being a project initiated by a group from within the Council rather than by agencies coming to the Council. In 1954, the Community Chest asked the Council to review the Gray House Guild's proposal to build a new convalescent hospital. The committee formed for this process gathered local information on needs as well as obtaining information from five other comparably sized cities across Canada. The results of this enquiry showed that Edmonton's population of older people was growing and that the services available left many gaps when compared with a balanced program.

After looking at the information derived from this study, an informal group of Council Board members began meeting with Bill Nicholls, the Executive Director in 1955, to look at 'problems of the aged'. This committee met with the whole Board of Directors on June 7, 1955 to request that a full scale study of the problems of the aged be conducted. In support of their proposal, Mrs. G.M. Cormie quoted from an outline of principles for the conduct of such studies published by the Community Chests and Councils of America:

1. Planning should be problem centered rather than agency or service centered. 'It is not enough to examine existing services on a one-by-one basis. Rather, the needs and problems of the aging should be defined in terms of broad fields of service or specific problem areas, that have meaning for people who have real concern for old folks . . . .'
2. All community forces having an interest in the problem should be invited to participate in planning for its solution.
3. Planning for the social needs of the aging must be integrated with overall community welfare planning through the Community Welfare Council.
4. The Council has a responsibility to inform and educate the community about the problems of the aging; to bring its knowledge and influence to bear on local, provincial, and national legislation; and otherwise to implement its recommendations and findings.

5. If planning for the aging is to go beyond peripheral problems to the meeting of basic needs, it involves investment of staff time to work with the necessary committees and related community groups and forces. (Minutes, Board of Directors, June 7, 1955)

The Board authorized a nucleus group to go ahead with the organization of such a study to examine issues such as housing, health, employment, recreation, and auxiliary services.

While this did not, perhaps, seem like a huge change of procedure at first, it was a first step toward centering its work and study on the citizens of the Edmonton community and their problems rather than on the work of the Edmonton agencies:

"That study was one of the first major studies done on seniors in all of Canada and we were very very proud of what we were doing. All the money for it was raised voluntarily. I remember we really sweated through that one. I left before it was completed to my chagrin. But I knew how much had gone into it. It was really a very exciting project. The idea was to find out from the older people themselves rather than to try to diagnose their problems. It was to be very specific in getting information . . . . That was a community development approach. It's premised on the idea that people know best what their problems are. It was part of our definite philosophy — that we wanted to find out from people themselves what their problems were, particularly with the seniors because we tend to stereotype that we have to do something for them." (Interview, Bill Nicholls, April 17, 1990)

This Study Committee on the Problems of the Aged proceeded with enthusiasm and developed a plan which included the preparation of a Directory of Services for the Elderly; a pilot project of intensive personal interviews conducted by trained social workers with 60 elderly people; a subsequent project of interviewing 1000 seniors, and finally an analysis of existing services to see how they corresponded to the needs. The committee drew up a budget of $3000 for the study, involved Board members such as Dr. Douglas Smith of the University Psychology Department in the development of a 150 question interview schedule, and proceeded. Over 700 interviews, lasting one and a half to two hours, were conducted by volunteers during 1956.

The committee planned to have an interim report on the survey ready by June of 1957. In fact, it took almost all of 1957, with most of the work being done by volunteers under the guidance of Dr. R. L. James from the University of Alberta. By the end of the year, a 155 page source book of facts about the elderly was produced, and the committee could celebrate the positive reactions of the social research community:

The redeeming feature of thorough work in the preparation of a source book is that independent social research specialists have assured us Edmonton has obtained a more intensive and useful source of information about the aging than has ever hitherto been achieved in this country; and the survey probably represents a closer view than has been obtained on any other segment of the population in Canada. (Annual Report, 1957)

At this point, unfortunately, the lack of staff resources on the Council began to hamper the study. Dr. James prepared several papers from the study data which he presented to professional sociological meetings in the U.S.A.; however, he was unable to produce an overall report from the findings until the sixties. Nevertheless, the data had been coded on IBM cards and thus special runs were able to be made to provide data on which to base a number of subsequent studies including studies on housing, convalescent hospitals, and dental health. In addition, it was effectively the first time in Edmonton, perhaps Canada, that the persons with the needs were consulted in a study of this scale. The committee itself noted the importance of this in its directions to Dr. James about the nature of the report which they hoped would be written:

One quality of the survey has been the approach of finding out, through the eyes of older people, what their needs and wants may be — it was thought this element should be preserved in the report wherever possible. Another thing which might be done is to dispel some of the myths which have grown up about circumstances of older persons. (Summary of meeting of Study Committee of the Aging, November 29, 1957).

Before the decade was out, this focus on the community was noted as a major change in the Council. It had started the decade by a name change which broadened its outlook from "social agencies" to "community services". In the 1959 Annual Report, G. S. Craig, President, summarized the changes in growth and approach which had occurred over the second decade of the Council's existence:

Our focus has changed fundamentally from a body primarily

concerned with inter-agency activities to one which deals with a range of undertakings related to a wide variety of community problems — from the broad base of the Youth Services Division to the needs and services for our senior citizens. It can well be said that your Council has endeavoured over the years to accept the challenge of change in a growing and expanding community.

Chapter Seven

A Central Focal Point

With major projects such as working with the rehabilitation committees, the refugee services, the Aging study, mental health services and transients, along with the organizational changes involved in amalgamating staff with the Community Chest, it might be assumed that the Council's plate was full. In fact, however, the issues that consumed an enormous amount of the Council's time and energy through the decade were the continuing issues of child welfare, and associated with that recreation and delinquency.

There were many services for children as the decade began, but they were of uncertain standards and represented ways of thinking about appropriate child care which belonged to the past. There were still, for example, several large orphanages run by private groups at a time when such institutional care was considered inadequate as well as out of date. Within the city, many of the services such as care of neglected children and of delinquents which are now associated with the province were then primarily the responsibility of the city. However, adoption — a central concern of the Whitton Report — remained a responsibility of the province. Subsidized day care was almost non-existent, provided only by the Edmonton Creche. In addition, there were a number of private day "foster homes", again of uncertain quality.

At the first meeting of the Child and Family Division in 1950, the issue of concern was the issue of training schools for delinquent boys. There were no training schools for delinquents at the time other than a small unit at Oliver Mental Institute which could accommodate 10 boys though with little training of any sort being offered. The Royal Commission had recommended that two training schools, one for younger and one for older children be built as soon as possible. The Division's discussion touched on many other needs of children, including day and boarding foster homes for children who were not wards of government. They were also concerned that there were no adequate facilities for non-delinquent but neglected children. By the end of the meeting, Division members agreed that a special committee should be appointed to,

> study the situation in some detail and bring back to a future meeting a report which would set forth the major needs in the child care field, and more particularly, facilities recommended for the care and training of juvenile delinquents. (Minutes, Child and Family Division, Feb. 21, 1950)

While this concern regarding training schools was under consideration, a crisis occurred in daycare. Begun during the war to assist mothers in war industries, the Edmonton Creche and Day Nursery, in the fifties, served primarily single mothers or mothers in families where a second income was required for survival. "Most of the mothers were employed in offices, stores, and restaurants, with some doing day work and factory sewing. Two thirds were earning $100 a month or less, and approximately one-third, $80 or less." (Minutes, Executive Committee, April 9, 1951). In the spring of 1951, the Creche was closed abruptly due to unsafe conditions. Stewart Bishop recalls the details:

> "There was a City Commissioner, John Hodgson, at the time, and he could be a dictator. One day I got a call from him, 'Bishop, get over here.' So I walked over, and he said 'I've just had an insurance agent tell me that they're removing the insurance on the building where the kids are kept.' This was an old building across from what was the police building and the reason the insurance company was cancelling the insurance was that gas was escaping and they thought the place was going to blow up. So Hodgson said, 'You better do something about it.'
>
> I thought 'Oh boy, twenty kids', and I said 'I'll have the financial support to do it?'
>
> 'Certainly, certainly. Do it,' he said.
>
> So I went back to the office and got the staff together and said 'we need 'x' number of day homes and we'll place these kids'. And this worked for a while." (Bishop, March 7, 1990)

The Creche building was an old city-owned building and had been provided free for many years. By this time, however, it was beyond repair. The City was prepared to provide alternative space, but none had been found. The Council took on the task of co-ordinating action to find a solution:

Following a visit to the Council office by a delegation of Creche mothers, it had been decided that the Council should convene a meeting of representatives of all groups and organizations concerned, in order that the total situation might be reviewed and plans made together regarding next steps . . . . Those present included representatives from the Creche Parents' Association, the Board of the Creche, the Community Chest, Council of Community Services, Civic Welfare Department, Family Service Bureau, and Aldermen Hanna and Tanner as unofficial representatives of City Council. (Minutes, Executive Committee, April 9, 1951)

The issue ultimately was one of money. The Board of the Creche had decided that it would not use makeshift quarters again. But the city's finances were in a difficult position, and the Creche Board did not feel that they could take on the task of fund-raising for a new building. The participants at the meeting agreed to keep in contact to try to find a solution.

It is important to note at this point some of the close relationships between the individuals working in the field. One of the most important relationships was that of Stewart Bishop to the Council. His Department, called the Civic Welfare Department by 1951, had offices on the ground floor of the old police building, while the Council and Chest shared the second floor. From the time Bishop arrived in Edmonton, he became an active member of the Child and Family Division and later joined the Board of the Council. At the same time, John Farina, the Superintendent of Recreation for the city and a trained social worker, was deeply involved in the Council's Group Work Division. He too was soon to be a member of the Council's Board. Throughout the fifties and early sixties these close collegial, but also personal, ties and friendships were at the base of much action in the social welfare field. As Stewart Bishop pointed out, the Council was a great deal of help to him in his role as Superintendent for the City Welfare as he was also able to help them. "The Council was the central focal point for solving many of these crises back then" (Interview, March 7, 1990) This collegiality did, in fact, play a role in solving the 1950's problems of the Creche, although other problems were to arise later:

"I [Stewart Bishop] was talking to the chap who was superintendent of recreation, John Farina, and I was frankly a little dubious about John Hodgson because he shouted so much. Farina said

'Oh, he barks at one end and wags at the other. Anything to do with kids, Stewart, you can get anything you want out of the guy'. So I finally said to Hodgson that the day homes were a temporary measure but we needed something permanent. So he put someone on it, next thing I know they've found a building. So it got started in the basement of a Pay-less Drug Store that was renovated and was quite a nice place." (Bishop, March 7, 1990)

Despite the new location for the Creche, The Child and Family Division of the Council felt that there was still considerable need for more investigation of the day and foster care situation as well as other child welfare needs, and in 1952, had established a Standing Committee of agencies on the whole area of child welfare. This Committee, and its various offshoots, carried on over the next several years to address many problems. After holding a Workshop on Child Welfare in 1953, for example, the Council brought together the seven child-care institutions to study the question of the rates of board $25/month paid to children's institutions by the province. Although this group was not made a formal committee of the Council, it was supported by Council staff. The group recommended a minimum rate of $35/month, and while there was no direct response, within six months there was an increase to $30/month granted.

Another study, this one begun in 1954 was of facilities for children who required care outside their homes, but were not wards of the government. At the time, placing of such children in foster homes was done largely by checking the classified ads for advertisements of foster home care. This included children who needed day care and children who needed temporary boarding care. Margaret Dick, Director of the Family Service Bureau wrote to the Council stating that her agency was concerned by the number of requests it had received for private placement of children without legal transfer of guardianship, and requesting a study:

It is certain that a number of children are being placed in Edmonton with very little inquiry as to the suitability of the foster parents and with little attention given to the possible effects on the child . . .

[As an example] Mrs. B. explained that she had three pre-school children for twenty-four hour care. One child was her own, the other two were boarding with her for a limited period. In addition, Mrs. B. explained, she kept from fifteen to twenty children under the age of six for day care. Infants and tiny tots were cared for on the main floor, the remaining older children played in a suite in the basement. She admitted she did not keep any help . . . Mrs. B. was genuinely unaware of any lack in her program or of any regulations to which she should be subject . . . .

How are these children fed? Who takes them to the bathroom? How can they get an undisturbed nap? Who comforts them when they are hurt or upset? Who helps settle a fight? All these questions arise immediately in this situation. In other cases, the inadequacies may not be so apparent though equally real and dangerous. (Brief on Foster Care, 1956)

This committee did an extensive study including interviews with some of those advertising foster care. On completion of the study, the Committee made several recommendations:

1. that a mere placement service to answer this need would not be an adequate solution
2. that the service be an all round, quality casework program offering homefinding and licensing, placement, counselling and supervision
3. that further study follow immediately on alternative services to placement, such as institutional care, homemaker's service and day care. (Brief on Foster Care, 1956)

Although licensing was not instituted, by 1957, the Committee had received a promise from the City to draw up a list of approved houses.

During the same years as these child welfare studies were taking place, the committee on delinquency — by this time made up of members of both the old Group Work and the Child and Family Division including Jack Anguish, Bill Pettigrew, Dr. Douglas Smith, Stewart Bishop, and John Farina — had split into three separate study committees looking at delinquency: the extent, description, and concentration of the problem; the existing services and their gaps and duplications; and information on methods of prevention and correction used in other centres. The entire group met in January 1955 to discuss their findings about the extent of delinquency. These showed that in 1954 there was a slight decline in delinquency over all, but that the number of girls who were running away was becoming an increasingly significant problem. Despite the decline in delinquency rates, the Board of the Council proposed that the review of existing services be carried out.

At this point, fate intervened in the form of Mayor Hawrelak, who was himself becoming concerned with the problems of delinquency. Again, Stewart Bishop describes the early activity behind the formation of the Youth Division of the Council:

"The Youth Services Division is an interesting story in itself. It started with the Mayor of Edmonton, Bill Hawrelak. It was at the time he was going through the city budget. Prior to talking to me, he had been talking to the Police Chief, and the Chief had been expressing a grave concern with the growth of gangs. He said that somebody ought to be doing something in a recreational-welfare sense. The police couldn't do anything after these kids got into trouble. The idea was to prevent it.

So Mr. Hawrelak suggested that maybe my Department had some responsibility and I expressed the view that it was a wider community problem since not only were the recreation department and the education department involved, there were the voluntary agencies, Boy Scouts, and Girl Guides, and Boys' Clubs, and other organizations that had to do with youth. And I recommended that we get the Executive Director of the Council, who was Jack Anguish at the time, and have a talk about it. Jack suggested that we have a conference which would bring all of these groups together to say what can we collectively do.

This made Mr. Hawrelak very nervous. He liked to know what things were going to happen before he was confronted with it. We had the meeting, I remember, in City Hall, and I was quite amused at how he nipped around from one group to another like he was a politician selling his party platform. After the meeting he was very elated. He came back and said 'It worked! Okay, now what do you fellows need?'

Well, we needed a worker in the Council who could guarantee there would be co-ordination of these agencies and get them together on a regular basis. So he said 'How much do you need?' I think we said something like $12,000. He just said 'Okay', and that was it." (Bishop, March 7, 1990)

It took several weeks from the time of the Mayor's first discussion with Stewart Bishop before the major meeting of all the groups involved could be arranged. In the meantime, Jack Anguish, Bill Nicholls — Assistant Director to the Council, and Stewart Bishop worked together in preparing the materials and the planning for the meeting.

The mayor's approach was to gather a panel of experts to present the case for a special committee for youth to the meeting, and then allow for discussion. Representatives from a wide range of organizations were invited, including police, education, court, private organizations, churches, public recreation, and service clubs. As Stewart Bishop noted, the meeting was a success and the Mayor's Advisory Committee on Youth Activities was organized. Bill Pettigrew was the chairman of the committee and Bill Nicholls, by that time Executive Director of the Council, acted as the secretary.

There was some debate within the Council at the time as to whether the Council was giving up some of its responsibility for co-ordinating services by participating in this co-ordinating committee of the Mayor's. However, those who took part in the Committee felt that the Mayor's involvement "made it possible to extend the base of support for coordination quite a measure beyond the groups normally associated with the Council". (Minutes, Management Committee of Council, Nov. 15, 1955) Certainly, Bill Pettigrew, President of the Council at the time, did not feel that the Council was in any way being usurped or bypassed:

"Bill Hawrelak was a very down-to-earth person. He tried to get into various aspects of the city, not to run it, but just to get a feeling. Now the Community Chest hadn't been too anxious that the Council people get together [with all the youth groups] because they felt that they might be ganged up on. Consequently, some of the things that we had been doing with youth groups had sort of fallen away and Bill [Hawrelak] felt this.

So he got a few of us together and said 'now, take a look at this [idea]. I'd like to help because some of these groups aren't getting good direction. I'd be willing to develop some city funds for them, develop some funds for a secretary.' So there were maybe twenty-five or thirty people there, and we got it down to seven members, and Bill Hawrelak said I would chair it. So we took a look at the whole thing for about three or four months

68

and then we decided that the best thing to do would be to make it some kind of adjunct to the Council.

We developed a Constitution and called people together, those interested in youth — we had about two hundred there — and they passed this Constitution. Then we got the money from the city, it was about $8000 per year. And we got a first class Secretary, David Critchley. He turned out to be a jewel." (Pettigrew, February 28, 1990)

By June of 1956, the Advisory Committee had prepared its proposal and brought it to the Board of Directors of the Council of Community Services on June 11. It was a major proposal, to add a Division for Youth which would have its own staff, Executive Committee, and its own separate funding. The Council accepted the idea, and thus, from 1956 until 1967, the Youth Division functioned as a semi-autonomous arm of Council.

In keeping with its role as a co-ordinating body, like the Council itself, the Division organized leadership training sessions, held regular meetings of youth workers, and developed a Directory of Youth Services, all in its first six months of operation. In the first three years of its operation, it was involved in many studies and projects. It carried out a survey of Boyle Street youth to see if there was a need for a Boys' Club, which it did recommend and help establish. It carried out a study of recreation services for the North-east Edmonton Community Council. In keeping with its origins, it created a study group on Delinquency Control and Prevention, and developed a brief for the Department of Justice. This brief contained 19 recommendations including the revision of the Juvenile Delinquents' Act, the expansion of the juvenile probation services, and the often repeated recommendation for the training and hiring of professional staff:

In most provinces, a certificate of proficiency is required by a barber before he is permitted to practice his skills on the exterior of one's head, but a similar certificate is not required for those treating the deep-seated emotional problems of children, and thus, in effect, work on the interior of one's cranium. We are of the opinion that more lasting effects are produced by psycho-therapy than by the techniques of the tonsorial practitioner, and that professional training, indeed, should be a pre-requisite for anyone endeavouring to do therapeutic work with children with emotional problems or with patterns of delinquency. (Brief prepared by the Delinquency Prevention and Control Study Group for the Department of Justice Committee on Juvenile Delinquency, 1958)

Like the Study on Aging, however, the Youth Division turned its attention to the actual user population as well as co-ordinating agency workers. It organized and sponsored a yearly Youth Conference. Then, in 1958, it organized a city-wide Teen Council which in the sixties was incorporated into the Division itself, giving youth a more direct voice in the organization. Thus, by the late fifties, there had been a number of accomplishments in the field of child welfare, and the Council itself now had one Division co-ordinating all of its activities in that area. Once again, however, a child welfare scandal would occur that would lead to the founding of yet another Council service.

Chapter Eight

Central Services and Information

The day-to-day life of the Council of Community Services included much more than the major studies and projects in which it was involved. There was, for instance, the question of premises. For much of the 1940s, the Council offices had been in the Tegler Building. Then, the Council moved, with the Community Chest, to the old police building on 98 street. Here, they were upstairs from the Civic Welfare Department, on the same floor as the Community Chest, and one floor down from the Oil and Gas Workers Union, whose leader also became a member of the Council's Board of Directors. The close physical arrangements facilitated the close collegial relationships of the staff of the various organizations. And while the building was not perfect, it had a unique character:

> "Of course, it [the building] had been a male-oriented building. But most of our staff was female, so they claimed the largest washroom which included three urinals. Miss Atkinson, who was secretary on the Chest side, was rather a stickler for proprieties, so on each of these urinals, there was a big pot of plants, you know the ones that tend to stream down in order to cover below." (Anguish, March 26, 1990)

The Civic Welfare Department, however, like so much else in Edmonton in the fifties, was growing. At one point, the Department started taking over the Council offices, one-by-one, and Jack Anguish found himself working in the joint Boardroom of Chest and Council. Then, with a new City Hall being built, it was decided that the Welfare Department would move there, leaving most of the police building available. The Council began to think in terms of developing a health and welfare building in which many agencies would share space and other resources. In 1955, the Council was given written assurance by the Mayor that the building would be available to it and other small agencies for a nominal rent. Negotiations had begun between several agencies and the Council, when it was announced that this building would, after all, be torn down. Instead, the Council and Chest were offered space in the Civic Block, leaving other agencies to make their own arrangements. Thus, in 1957, first the Chest and then the Council moved to the sixth floor of the Civic Block on 99 Street. Several smaller agencies did find space ultimately in the Civic Block, thus moving some way toward the staff's dream of a health and welfare centre.

Being employees of both Council and Chest meant that staff spent considerable time working on Chest business, especially during the autumn funding campaign each year. In addition, the Council worked as a kind of assessment arm of the Community Chest, doing evalua-tions of Chest agencies and studying new agencies which applied for Chest funding. Thus, during the first half of the fifties, the staff studied the Emergency Housekeeper Service, the John Howard Society, the Canadian Arthritis and Rheumatism Society, In-the City Camps, and the SPCA and Pound on the request of the Chest. They also did a major study of the Home for Ex-Servicemen's Children. This was an orphanage which wished to expand; however, in keeping with the Council's views on the need for more foster homes rather than large children's institutions, the study recommended that the Home reduce numbers instead. Then in 1956, the Chest Budget Committee asked that detailed reviews of all Chest Agencies be done:

> With the rapid expansion of Edmonton has come a need for existing social welfare organizations to plan ahead for inevitable demands for services . . . . In 1956, the Budget Committee of the Community Chest expressed the need for more facts on possible expansion of services as well as further knowledge of the adequacy of existing services.
>
> The Board of Directors of the Community Chest has therefore asked the Council for reviews of agency services. The reviews were asked to cover such matters as: analysis of present services, possible future expansion, capital expenditures, non-Chest revenues, and coordination with other services. As it is a tremen-dous task to cover 31 agencies it was proposed that a few agen-cies be taken each year, concentrating on agencies providing similar services. (Annual Report, 1956)

The first of these detailed agency reviews was done in 1956, on the Edmonton Creche and Day Nursery Society, and proved to be an enormous task:

A special committee was set up to conduct a review with one of the member agencies. An appraisal of the approach taken showed it would be impossible for the Council to conduct as intensive studies with all agencies. It is thought now informational reports might be prepared with much less effort and still provide the Budget Committee with useful and up-to-date information for their purposes. (Annual Report, 1957)

Thus, most reports in future years, such as a report on Camps, and on the Hope Mission's request for admission to the Chest were less intensive.

As well as the work of and for the Community Chest, the Council operated several "central" services, including the publication of the Directory of Services, the Christmas Bureau, and the Social Service Exchange. All three of these had begun in 1940 with the Council itself. The Directory of Services, with much effort by volunteer committee members as well as staff, was revised and re-published every two years to give agencies, and other concerned Edmontonians, an up-to-date list of the social services in town.

The Christmas Bureau was also run primarily by a volunteer committee with help from existing Council staff. It was 1959 before a full-time person was hired for the six weeks of the Christmas rush. As early as the mid-1940s, Council members began discussing the relationship of Christmas giving to year-round charity, and feeling a certain sense of unease with encouraging the once-a-year gift-giving. Nevertheless, the Christmas Bureau operated successfully as part of the Council right through to 1970s, when it became an incorporated as a separate organization. Even then, it operated out of Council offices with extensive assistance from Council staff until the mid 1980s.

The Social Service Exchange was not so successful. Even in the beginning, only a portion of the agency members of the Council became members of the Social Service Exchange. There was always a question in workers' minds about the possibility of violating confidentiality through the Exchange, although nothing more than names, ages, and addresses were ever recorded in the Exchange. The Provincial Public Welfare Department would not use the Exchange because there was a provision in the Welfare Act prohibiting any disclosure about cases, including names. By the mid-fifties, use had declined substantially despite considerable efforts by the Social Service Exchange Committee, headed by Mrs. G. Sparling, to encourage agencies to use it. In 1956, the committee carried out an agency self-study. The results were not encouraging:

The major reasons for this trend [declining use of Exchange] are (a) A change in casework philosophy; (b) Information has become readily available from clients; (c) Staff time involved in the registration process, was not in proportion to the value derived. (Annual Report, 1956)

The Committee recommended a suspension of Exchange operations for a year with the hope that agencies would make notes of any times when they could have been helped by the Exchange. In addition,

As a partial compensation for the lack of a Social Service Exchange, the committee further recommended that the Board of Directors study the possibilities of establishing a broader and more comprehensive information and referral service. (Annual Report, 1956)

The Council Board of Directors did suspend operations of the Exchange in 1957 and again in 1958, and began a study into the need for and development of an information service. Subsequent events in the community provided the impetus for the relatively speedy development of such a service:

"There was a soldier stationed at Griesbach who used to beat his kid. One day he hit him too hard and killed him. This became a public scandal, and Mr. Hooke, who was Minister of Municipal Affairs, made a public statement that there should be a Bureau to Prevent Cruelty to Children. At this point, I picked up the phone and phoned Mr. Hagen [Deputy Minister of Welfare] and said 'For God's sake, doesn't he know that the Provincial Welfare Department is responsible for neglected children?'

The next thing I know, we have a long series of discussions about this. Mr. Hooke had to somehow get off the hook. He claimed that 75,000 letters came in on the issue. So they decided to have a large meeting at which there were 125 people from [different organizations]. One of the things that came up was that we were not aware of problems like this. There was no way of knowing.

If the wife or the neighbours had known where to get information [the death might not have happened]. So access to information became a critical issue.

Mr. Hooke said, 'We need a welfare information service. How
are we going to do it? I'll guarantee you'll get $60,000 to set it up.'

At that point — we had some plans already in mind — we said,
'It has to be community-wide, not just government based'. They
thought of it simply as a government hot-line. We said, 'No, this
thing involves all of the voluntary agencies. This problem exists
in all of the agencies, not just the child welfare field.' The result
was that we created a tripartite financial arrangement where the
city paid a third, the province paid a third, and the Council of
Community Services carried the other third and administered [the
information service]. It was eventually spun off and became an
organization in its own right and now has become a very
sophisticated computerized service." (Bishop, March 7, 1990)

The beating of the child at Griesbach took place in the autumn of 1958,
and the Council's first reaction to it was to have the Youth Services
Division do a study of Minister Hooke's proposal for a Society for
the Prevention of Cruelty to Children. The Division decided to hold
hearings on the issue, inviting representatives of City and Provincial
Welfare, Edmonton Police Force, Juvenile Court, and Family Service
Bureau. In addition, a survey was conducted on the same day as the
hearings 'to determine public knowledge of and attitude towards
existing child protection services'. Two conclusions of the hearings
and survey were of particular importance:

Your Committee feels that there is a serious lack of knowledge
on the part of the public as to the facilities available and the laws
that apply with regard to neglect cases.

There would appear to be a portion of the public which fails to
report cases of neglect either because of lack of confidence in those
charged with responsibility for child protection and their failure
to follow up complaints, or because they have heard that their
identity will be revealed, or they feel that they will meet with
a hostile or indifferent reception. Your Committee feels that this
is another question that requires further study. (Report of Special
Committee on Child Protection, January 22, 1959)

Simultaneous with these hearings and public survey, another Council committee, the Information and Referral study group, which had been formed a year and a half earlier, produced the results of its survey and provided the Council with three recommendations which it was then able to take to the meetings with the province:

1. That a Central Information and Referral Service be established in Edmonton.
2. That this service be attached to the Edmonton Council of Community Services; . . .
3. That the establishment of such a service be accompanied by extensive publicity, and that a program of concentrated public education be part of this service on an ongoing basis.(Minutes, Board of Directors, Jan. 12, 1959)

The provincial sub-committee, which consisted of Deputy Minister Hagen, Stewart Bishop, and Bill Nicholls, reviewed the Council's reports on both child protection and information and referral, and developed a five-point plan which the province subsequently accepted. The Council was asked, and agreed, to set up such a centre. Various committee volunteers examined such information centres as were run across the country and brought back information as to the specific nature of the task:

Mrs. Collier said she had spoken with the staff person at the Toronto Information and Referral Centre operated by the Social Planning Council in Toronto and learned that a professionally qualified person was definitely required as frequently the job was to discover the real nature of the problem presented.(Minutes, Board of Directors, March 9, 1959)

By October of 1959, the province and Council had agreed on the objects and general operational principles of what was now named the Welfare Information and Referral Service:

Objects of Service
1) To provide promptly and accurately welfare information and referral for the Edmonton region
2) To record information on the nature of the information requested and referrals made.
3) To provide an up-to-date file of welfare information on agency service, showing policies and conditions upon which services are rendered.

4) To make the service known thoroughly to the general public and to the private agencies and governmental departments concerned.
5) The extent of the information to be provided would cover a broad interpretation of welfare. Determination of the scope of information and referral would be worked out by the advisory committee for the service. (Memorandum from W.M. Nicholls to Council, October 26, 1959)

Thus, though the Welfare Information and Referral Service would for its first six to eight weeks of operation deal only with child welfare questions, while staff attended to setting up the service, it was designed as the broad welfare service which the Council had envisioned. Thelma Scambler, former head of the Central Volunteer Bureau, was hired and the service moved into operation on June 15, 1960.

Another of the important Council activities that could be considered a central service was education. Right from the beginning, the Executive Directors had given speeches to many community organizations as well as giving various lecture series to university classes such as the nursing department. In addition, the Council had been involved in developing and encouraging social welfare courses given through the Faculty of Extension at University of Alberta.

The work of public education had always been associated with the work of the public relations committee of the Council. As early as 1943, the Council felt the need to develop a greater public understanding of its work and the work of other agencies. One of its first attempts was a series of four radio plays, carried by CJCA and CFRN, on particular agencies. The most successful was "The Light Changed" written by the well-known Edmonton playwright, Gwen Pharis Ringwood, for the Institute for the Blind.

By the mid-fifties, there was a major effort being made in the public education field. It was felt that the more the public and the growing range of agencies knew about social welfare issues and techniques, the more the work of the Council itself would be understood and valued. A regular newsletter was published and several types of education meetings were held:

"Twice a year we had training sessions for various kinds of work. And instead of having an Annual Meeting, we used to try to enliven it and get a wider range, so that the people who came to it would feel a part of it and also be trained in new ways of doing things, how to get to the heart of the matters, that kind of thing." (Pettigrew, February 28, 1990)

Starting in 1956, the Council held three annual Fall Institutes on matters that were of concern to the social welfare community. The 1956 Institute *"Teamwork in our Growing City"* had both public relations and public education purposes:

> ... as a general meeting of the Council of Community Services it would bring together delegates from a great variety of community groups and agencies, volunteer and professional workers, and persons from public departments and from private organizations. Such a gathering might not only help cement the bonds among community groups, but also help bring about the realization [that] the Council is the aggregate of community organizations represented by their delegates. It might, above all, bring out the increased recognition of the importance of the cooperation of all in meeting the social Welfare problems in our Community.(Proceedings of Fall Institute, 1956)

That first Institute brought Professor William Dixon from the University of British Columbia's School of Social Work as the keynote speaker. There were seven workshops: "The Unmarried Mother", "Delinquent Youth or Delinquent Parents", "Where are we going in Rehabilitation?", "Family Stress in Modern Society", "More Children, But Whose Responsibility?", "The Transient Problem", and "Social Effects of Industrial Expansion". This format, of guest speaker and a variety of workshops was continued for the next two Institutes, and was met with considerable enthusiasm from the community, despite the holding of the 1958 Institute on the day of a big Edmonton Eskimo football game. Perhaps one of the most important aspects of these institutes was that as well as using people from the university and social agencies as speakers and resource people, they also drew heavily on the overall community, including business and labour, thus again broadening the range of people involved with Council issues.

Finally, in looking at the development of the Council itself over the period of the 1950s, it is important to look at the changes made to the Council's Constitution in order to follow the way in which trends in the work became part of the accepted nature of the Council. With the reorganization of the Council in 1952 and the amalgamation of staff with the Community Chest, there were several changes to the

Constitution. These changes were structural. They eliminated the Divisions, created a Board of Directors, elected by the membership, to run the organization. They also eliminated the various classes of membership which the first Constitution had included based on the particular type of agency which was applying.

There was, also, a desire to include more than structural changes in the Constitution. This finally culminated in an new Constitution with new objects in 1957:

1. To facilitate cooperation among all welfare, health and recreational services in the community.
2. To facilitate cooperation of organizations in planning their work to meet the social welfare needs of the community, present, and future.
3. To facilitate cooperative action in matters of social welfare improvements and the development of an informed public opinion on social welfare problems.
4. To study existing services and recommend methods of improving, extending, and preventing duplication of services.

These objects illustrate the way in which Council thinking had been changing as reflected by the move from the central function being co-ordination of agencies to the central function being the facilitation of co-operation between agencies and other groups. Objective three, in particular, points to the fact that the Council, as it had grown in staff and budget, had also grown in its conception of a constituency to include, by this time, the whole of the social welfare community. Thus, by 1959, the twentieth anniversary of its formation, the Council of Community Services could congratulate itself on being accepted by the Community Chest, the voluntary agencies, city departments, and increasingly by provincial departments as a central piece in the social welfare puzzle in Edmonton. The events of the next decade were about to challenge that centrality.

Summary

1950 - 59: Transition and Growth

If the 1940's were years of initiative-taking, the 1950s were the years when the Council became a major force in the Edmonton social welfare establishment. Edmonton itself was experiencing an economic boom associated with expansion of resource activities in the north and the development of the oil industry. The Council changed its name to the Council of Community Services in 1950 reflecting the expansion of its own range of concerns.

Then, with staff working for both the Community Chest and the Council, and with some Council Directors also being City employees in the human service areas, the Council became the central organization for resolving social crises. It acted as the focal point, bringing together diverse interest groups in the areas of transients, rehabilitation, youth, and information to create new organizations to fill social welfare gaps. As the decade went on, the Council was looked to even by the provincial government as the agency which could pull together voluntary and government forces to solve problems. These problems included the information gap demonstrated by the Griesbach child battering scandal which resulted in the formation of the Welfare Information Service.

As well as playing this leading liaison role for the voluntary and government social sectors, the Council was beginning to listen to a new constituency — the people who themselves had the problems and concerns. With the Study on Aging as well as some of the work with teens, the Council committed itself to be a voice both for and with the whole community. This commitment would result in major changes in its activities, focus, and position in the community over the next two decades.

Section Three
1960 – 69:
Changing Voices

Chapter Nine

A New Outlook, A New Shape

One of the difficulties of serving the social welfare needs of the Edmonton community in the later 1950s was the growing number of funding appeals which were being made outside of the Community Chest, particularly by large national health organizations such as the Red Cross, Crippled Children, and the Canadian National Institute for the Blind (CNIB). Not only were some of these national campaigns competing with the Community Chest for dollars, but there were also several instances of organizations competing with each other. For example, in July 1957, Bill Nicholls received a letter from the CNIB complaining of a campaign being planned by a rival, the Canadian Federation of the Blind:

> It has come to our attention that the Canadian Federation of the Blind is presently planning and conducting a Province-wide campaign in Alberta for the announced purpose of establishing training and rehabilitation services to be located centrally in the Province. According to our information the campaign objective is $300,000.

> In view of the fact that The Canadian National Institute for the Blind in Alberta has a Province-wide programme in operation designed to meet the essential needs of blind people of all ages, races and creeds it would seem that no new facilities could be established which would not duplicate existing facilities and services . . . .

> In all of this I would like to emphasize that our Organization is concerned solely with providing the highest standard of essential services to all blind people while at the same time avoiding unnecessary demands upon public generosity through working for the elimination and prevention of duplication. The strong emotional appeal of blindness makes it relatively simple for

independent groups having little or no regard for community planning and co-ordination to meet with a measure of success in fund-raising efforts in the name of the blind.(W.E. Milton, Superintendent, Alberta Division, CNIB, July 10, 1957)

In response, the Chest and Council formed a small committee of two members from each to investigate the problem. It soon became apparent that there were many organizations canvassing for funds, and that some of these were of an uncertain nature:

Mr. Bruce then raised the question of the organization known as the United Welfare Organization and asked Mr. W. Nicholls if he could supply information.

Mr. Nicholls said that a Rev. Fox seemed to be the key person in the organization and that its history had been very questionable. At one time the organization operated a cafe for persons without means, and solicitations had been obtained from business concerns. The cafe had subsequently been closed by the Health Department. Rev. Fox's wife had taken him to court for non-support and an associate who had backed the project had been committed to Oliver. For a time nothing was heard of the United Welfare Organization but recently a campaign was started to raise funds for a building.(Minutes, Joint Meeting of Community Chest Executive Committee and Edmonton Council of Community Services Management Committee, February 19, 1958).

At the same time as this committee was investigating the immediate situation of multiple appeals in Edmonton, there was a wave of interest in United Funds sweeping across Canada from the United States. In 1957, the Community Chests and Councils Division of the Canadian Welfare Council began a concerted study into the effects of this new instrument of fund-raising on the work of Councils. The study group listed the following as characteristics of the situation in cities where Funds were beginning:

- [United Fund] trend similar to earlier one out of which developed Chests.
- Entry into voluntary partnership of national agencies, inexperienced in joint community planning.
- Entry and influence of a new leadership, inexperienced in planning, from economic power group.

- 'Open door' policy, a two-edged sword, can mean inclusion of duplicating or poor quality services.
- Growing awareness of welfare services on part of public.
- Growing voice of outlying areas regarding services and campaigns.
- Lack of status of planning organizations compared to fund-raising organizations.
- Shortage of lay and professional leadership in planning.
- Undefined roles of laymen and professionals in planning.
- Inadequacy of research and planning by councils and chests.
- Lack of clarity of local, regional and national obligations. (Sub-committee on Social Planning in United Fund Cities, Councils Section, Community Chests and Councils Division, Canadian Welfare Councils, July 1957)

The United Fund movement, like the earlier Community Chest movement, was largely a response to the multiplicity of funding appeals. It, however, intended to bring together a much broader cross-section of society. The earlier movement had brought local social and health agencies together with business. The new Funds intended to include labour in a major way and to add all the national agencies to their fund-raising federation. They also intended to move toward an efficient business-model in fund-raising, involving the most prestigious business men in each city as their volunteers.

It was, perhaps, partly the emphasis on big business and big prestige which raised concern among Councils across the country. Many Councils were amalgamated with Community Chests and familiar with working primarily on the local level. There was apprehension that a large fund-raising organization, possibly dominated by national organizations, would overwhelm the smaller local organizations, including the Councils. At the same time, it was noted that there would be an increased need for planning as the scope of the organizations grew, but the Councils foresaw the possibility of being swallowed by the Funds:

The weakness of financial dependency on the fund-raising body are obvious and all too apparent to the missionaries serving in the Council field. As the amount raised by the federation establishes a certain percentage available for central services, the limits of development of any one Council are fairly well established. In larger centers this may pose no great concern; but in smaller cities, lack of sufficient funds available for Council purposes is a telling problem. Financial dependency upon the fund-raising organization also creates a situation where the Council may be placed in the position of being simply a social planning arm of the fund-raising colossus.(Straw Man Paper: Financing of Councils, Canadian Welfare Council, 1957)

With such concerns being voiced across the country, it is not surprising that the Edmonton Chest and Council took a very low key stance when, in 1958, a group from the Chamber of Commerce began to study the possibility of creating an Edmonton United Fund:

An informal discussion was held on the Council's responsibility in relation to the possible development of a United Fund in Edmonton. It was agreed the Council like the Chest was not in a position to spearhead any development of a United Appeal. (Minutes, Board of Directors, February 9, 1959)

Nevertheless there was a concern about the relationship of the Council to a United Fund that led to the establishment of a study group consisting of Mrs. H.B. Collier, Douglas Homersham, Bill Nicholls, and Stewart Bishop. This group led the Council Board through several discussions of the Council's future before arriving at a position. The United Community Fund (UCF) was incorporated in February 26, 1960. The Council organized a special Institute January 13, 1960 for Council members to discuss the Fund and to help the Board develop an official position. By the end of January,they had developed that position:

1. As the Edmonton Council of Community Services has a social welfare planning responsibility both within and outside the field of federation of voluntary organizations the Council should:
   a) Retain its separate identification as a social planning body — i.e. separate purposes and by-laws, membership, board of directors and its own budget.
   b) Seek to establish a close working relationship with the United Community Fund so as to act with authority and defined responsibility in areas where social planning and research are related to financing. Such areas would include:
   1) Power to appoint 1/2 membership of United Community Fund Allocations Committee.

2) An inter-change of board members with United Community Fund — (3-6 members) — to include members
of executive committees of both organizations.
3) To establish service criteria and evaluation procedure
required for the admission of new agencies to the United
Community Fund and to conduct reviews with a view
to determining eligibility for membership. Such procedures would also be used to test the validity of existing
membership.
4) To study and recommend on all United Community Fund
agency requests for capital campaigns.
2. That the Council continue present joint-staffing arrangements
with United Community Fund and receive financial support
adequate to the responsibility of carrying out its functions. (A
Statement on Council's Relationship to Proposed United Community Fund, January 20, 1960)

The arrangements with the Fund were not concluded smoothly,
however. The Council held a general meeting of its members on March
14th at which its position and a motion that the Council join the United
Community Fund was presented to delegates. The insecurity of many
agencies became evident at that meeting:

It was evident planning for the meeting had not taken fully into
account the amount of hostility represented by the questions raised
at the meeting. The hostility seemed to represent:
a) Concern about the idea of the United Community Fund
— that the agency might become lost — particularly the
smaller one.
b) Personal mischief-making type of hostility.
c) A fear of the national health organizations.
(Minutes, Management Committee, March 18, 1960)

The Management Committee of the Council quickly agreed that
another general meeting would have to be held at which these fears
were dealt with. The questions raised at the March 14 meeting were
subsequently answered in an extended memo to Council members,
and the Council did join the Fund, but not without some reservations
as Douglas Homersham, President of the Council in 1961, expressed:

"At that time, there was a transfer of responsibilities occurring
from the financial end of the Council operations and the social

planning aspect of it . . . . The financial planning, the question of one appeal for all organizations, how effective this was going to be, was very important. Would all of the different organizations be members of the United Way or wouldn't they? There was a lot of sorting out to do and a lot of development. Of course, history has proven now that one organization hasn't been sufficient to take care of everybody.

It was not a smooth change, not at all. They [the UCF] were looked upon with a question mark as a lot of things are until you prove yourself. And then, there were such organizations as the Red Cross that couldn't come in." (Interview, Douglas Homersham, March 13, 1990)

Once the Fund was established, the Council and Fund formed a joint committee to begin to discuss the specifics of their relationship. What became apparent in these discussions was a clear difference in purposes, which had been anticipated, and a consequent difference in staff criteria, which had not been anticipated. The three major staff of the Council/Chest were Bill Nicholls, Executive Director; Gustave deCocq, Research Director; and David Critchley, Executive Secretary of the Youth Division. All of these men had strong backgrounds in social work and social research, but none had backgrounds in fundraising other than their work with the Edmonton Community Chest. Nevertheless, the Council Board was in favour of the joint staffing at that point:

"I felt that the joint staff arrangement was the most effective way because they were close to both the financial aspect and the social planning aspect. When the UCF came into being there was a great deal of concern that the financial planning operation would be on a pedestal by itself, if I may put it that way. [After the separation of staff] I think there wasn't the integration that there was when they were combined. That is still my feeling about it, that you can't divorce one from the other." (Homersham, March 13, 1990)

The Board members of the new Fund were not convinced of the value of the joint staffing arrangements, and certainly were not prepared to begin their first campaign without a professional fund raiser. Thus, for the first campaign, they added such a professional fund raiser to the joint staff.

Within the first few months of the Fund's existence, however, it appeared that the joint staffing arrangement was no longer appropriate. The upshot was that in December, 1960 the Council and the Fund severed their connection. This included a complete separation of staffing, although they each continued to appoint members to the other's Board. The separation had some positive effects for the Council:

"The transition of the Chest into the Fund was a time of a great deal of excitement. I guess it was nascent growth and growing pains. Under a lot of pressures and changes that occurred, the staff was divided between the Fund and Council. . . . It really set the stage then for the Council to pursue its own independent activities. It expanded the opportunities . . ." (Nicholls, April 17, 1990)

The separation, also however, raised some immediate problems. The first problem rose around the issue of space. With the separation of staff, it became apparent that the space available to the Council was insufficient, and became even more so during campaign periods. In addition, the offices were, at that time, on the third floor of the Royal Bank Building, a building without an elevator, and thus were not wheel-chair accessible. On Dec. 27, 1960 the Management Committee noted:

There is no longer the necessity of retaining joint premises and in some respects the re-location of the Council offices to other premises would help to secure the separate identification of the Council with its concerns for joint planning in the areas of public as well as voluntary services. (Minutes)

The Council proceeded to hunt for, and locate, separate space in the Clarke Building on 103 Street. The problem, then, arose of leaving the United Fund with space which it did not need except during the campaign. The Council did move to 10011-103 Street, but only after extensive negotiations with both the Fund and the bank on subletting the former Council space.

A more serious problem arose when the Council submitted its budget to the Fund in the winter of 1961. The Fund did not approve the total Council budget and set out its response as follows:

The first [point] is this; the Directors of the United Community Fund have a strong conviction that there is a primary need in this community for a competent Council of Community Services to carry out a continuous appraisal of human needs in the community, and to recommend strongly the methods by which these needs can be met in the most efficient and humane manner. Secondly, that no health or welfare agency or function, however meritorious it may be, can advance much beyond its acceptance in the community. The Executive of the Fund feels that active consideration should be given by your Board of Directors to a more clear interpretation to the public of the actual work and services performed for the community by the Edmonton Council of Community Services . . . .

After exhaustive consideration, the Directors of the United Community Fund approved the appropriation to the Council of Community Services to continue for a period of forty-five days from this date at the rate of $50,439.00 annually as previously appropriated, and the appropriation for the balance of 1961 was approved at the rate of $38,280.00 annually. (Minutes, Board of Directors, May 1, 1961)

As a consequence of the separation from the Fund, the Council Board had already decided to do a thorough agency self-study. Now, it threw itself into preparing a shorter budget analysis in order to meet the Fund's forty-five day extension of the higher rate of funding. Bettie Hewes, then a Council appointee to the Fund Board, reported on her sense of the most appropriate tactics:

Mrs. Hewes felt it was imperative we do not get into a defensive position on this matter; indeed there was a good chance to capitalize on the situation by explaining what the Council is all about. She didn't think the Fund Board was against the Council but that there was some lack of communication. She felt the presentation should be prepared for the Fund Board meeting in concise point form indicating what we have accomplished and what our plans are for the future. (Minutes, Board of Directors, May 1, 1961)

The Council produced an eight page, point-form listing of its projects, and with that were able to renegotiate the 1961 budget with the Fund, just prior to beginning negotiations on the 1962 budget. Subsequently, they were also able to negotiate an agreement with the Fund which reflected the Council's thinking that,

. . . the scope of the work of the Council was broader than that of the Fund as it reflected a different type of membership, and 2) The Council has a special relationship as a planning organization with the Fund. (Minutes, Executive Committee, Sept. 6, 1961)

Thus, after almost two years of negotiation, it seemed that the Council's relationship with the new United Community Fund had stabilized.

What may have been even more important to the Council than these negotiations with the Fund, however, was the intense self-analysis which Board and staff engaged in during those same years to determine the Council's direction. Under the chairmanship of Bill Pettigrew, and later Dr. Julius Guild, psychiatrist and Council Board Member, the Council undertook a three-part self-study. Part One of the study covered the Council's current resources in terms of staff, finances, and volunteers, noting both the good quality of staff and volunteers, and the minimum resources with which they were working. Part Two of the Report, delivered in October 1961, used twelve criteria for self-evaluation taken from a publication of the United Community Funds and Councils of America, "Guideposts for Effective Community Planning." These criteria dealt with matters such as the quality of volunteer citizen participation, council structure, the need for research "and honest conviction" as the basis for positions taken, services to both voluntary and tax-supported agencies, long range planning, relationships to provincial and national agencies, public education, the need to relate social planning to physical planning, and financing.

The observations of the self-study committee regarding the Council's operation in respect to these twelve criteria led to Self-study, Stage Three, and a series of recommendations made to the Board in February 1962. The main recommendations included structural recommendations such as to continue to broaden the representativeness of the Board, to form an advisory Board of people to reach into "the top levels of leadership in the community", to improve public relations, and to broaden funding sources. The recommendations also suggested some changes in emphasis in the focus of the Council's activities:

The Executive Committee believes that the future development of the Council should increasingly emphasize the functions of social welfare planning . . . .

The Executive Committee agreed resources of the Council should be allocated specifically and not 'spared' for research and long range planning. (Council Self Study - Stage III)

At the same time as this self-study was taking place, the Council was also writing a new constitution to take into account the separation from the Fund. Seeing itself in the sharp focus of the United Community Fund's objectives seems to have encouraged the Council to make the broadening of its thought and membership explicit in the new set of by-laws approved at the 1961 Annual Meeting, particularly in the new objects:

The objects of the Council of Community Services of Edmonton and District are:

1. To contribute to the general well-being of the residents of the community by planning, developing, and instituting, in cooperation with interested individuals, agencies, organizations, and departments of all levels of government, effectual, efficient and adequate programs for the attainment and maintenance of the highest practical standards in the provision of health, welfare and recreational services.

2. To provide a vehicle and a nucleus for facilitating the cooperation by, and division of responsibilities between, its member organizations and departments in establishing and discharging their respective responsibilities.

3. To survey, examine and analyze and report upon the social needs of the community . . . for the purpose of assessing and evaluating the adequacy, effectiveness and efficiency of the services then provided, and when necessary initiate and/or assist in the provision of new and/or additional services.

4. To encourage and facilitate cooperation among all social agencies, organizations and departments serving the community . . .

5. To institute and execute a continuing program of public education . . .

6. To cooperate with and give assistance to The United Community Fund of Greater Edmonton and other fund-raising organizations and interested departments of all levels of government by study, analysis, research, evaluation and reports and recommendations . . .

7. To carry out research and conduct experiments in all or any fields or areas of social service either at the request of any member agency, organization or department, The United

Community Fund of Greater Edmonton, or on its own initiative, and in particular to conduct such studies and/or research as may be necessary in order to anticipate the future needs of the community or to prevent, control or find solutions to any social problem.

These objectives indicate the distance the Council had moved from the original Council of Agencies and the extent to which it was now prepared to move on particular social problems on its own initiative. According to Bettie Hewes, President of the Council in 1962 and 1963, these objectives also reflected the beginning of change in the views of members of the Board on the core importance of what they were doing:

"The Board was made up of good folk who represented the backbone of the community and cared about the circumstances of the community, but we really weren't terribly well versed in stimulating major change and we didn't see that as our role. We changed our name at that point to the Edmonton Welfare Council because we believed that we had a primary function to care for those who were helpless and hopeless, and there seemed to be evidence that they were out there and not being attended to. There was a beginning anxiety that we had too long been simply a Council of Agencies and had spent a lot of our energy protecting the status quo, which was good and functioning and operating, but that our role needed to move out of that." (Interview, Bettie Hewes, February 5, 1990)

The President's Report in the 1963 Annual Report confirmed the evolution which the Council experienced over the first three years of the sixties:

The first thing we did last year on the direction of the Annual Meeting was to change our name. A small mechanical detail perhaps — but symptomatic of a much deeper change which has taken place gradually. Becoming the Edmonton Welfare Council gave us a new outlook, a new shape, it put an end firmly to an old era and gave our changed philosophy legal status. We are no longer a Council of services but a Council for welfare and changing our name stated once and for all that we are prepared to act like one. (President's Report, 1963)

One of the most crucial aspects of this "deeper change" was indicated later in this same report:

In recent years we know the Council has experienced a change in philosophy and this has been accompanied by a change in procedure, gradual but strong and healthy and still growing . . . . At the risk of getting tangled in terminology this method is described as community development — let's talk about it. Social work in general and community organization in particular have concentrated on improving conditions and simultaneously strengthening the individual in his environment. Community development seems to take that necessary step beyond this and attempts to reshape and reconstruct the environment so that fewer people will be broken in the future or require strengthening. This is accomplished through the joint efforts of the people most closely involved; the goals are determined by the people, and the process is cooperative.

Al Affleck, Chairman of the Activities Committee which was responsible for much of the work with members including education and recruiting of a broadening membership during this period, reflects on his sense of what the Council's changed approach meant:

"I taught courses for several years that talked about community development. It seems to me it's basically about getting people together to try to make democracy work. It's a process of problem identification and problem solving, or partial problem solving, developing productive kinds of relationships between different kinds of subgroups in the community. And the literature in all these fields [social work, recreation, community development] have something to do with fostering creativity on the part of the individual, bringing out the best in groups, getting communication going between groups . . . .

I felt that there was a parallelism between various kinds of social organizational principles and what the Council was doing. I was impressed that every now and again, someone would take two or three or four points as a principle, the kind of principles you find when you read certain books on community development and community problem solving. The fact is that better than any other group that I was ever involved with, there seemed to be those kind of principles guiding the group." (Interview, A. F. Affleck, March 7, 1990)

This period of the early sixties was an era in which people had begun to look for change. Working for and improving your democracy had been given an air of dignity and nobility through John Kennedy's "Ask not what your country can do for you, but what you can do for your country" inaugural speech and Martin Luther King's passionate "I have a dream" speech. The Edmonton Welfare Council, now a separate and distinct organization, seems to have felt a part of that movement of democratic idealism, and begun the work of developing its own sense of identity as a major agent of change.

Chapter Ten

Planning — For and With Youth

While the Council was changing in structure and in its own self-definition, its focus of concern in the community did not change so much as enlarge. For the first half of the sixties, it functioned as a two-part organization, with the Youth Division dealing with all issues related to youth while the Council continued its work in relation to issues such as services for seniors, rehabilitation services, and services to transients. The Youth Services Division, either alone or in conjunction with the Executive Committee of the Council, took on or continued a wide variety of projects, each of which showed evidence of the Council's growing concern with "the basic question of whether we are planning with or for people". (Annual Report, 1961).

The role of the Council in examining day care services provides a good example of the way that Council work grew. In the summer of 1960, the subject of day care was raised again through concern about the recurring issue of appropriate space for the Creche, still the only subsidized day care in Edmonton:

> Mr. Homersham reported . . . 'Within a year the facilities presently used by the Edmonton Creche will no longer be available. Besides the problem of re-location of the Creche it is apparent that the need for day care services for children in Edmonton needs to be investigated'. (Minutes, Board of Directors, September 12, 1960)

A joint committee of Council and Youth Division representatives was set up to investigate day care throughout the community in voluntary and commercially operated institutions as well as the Creche. This committee held discussions with the city and the Provincial Welfare Department in respect to the quality of day care legislation. The University Women's Club carried out one survey of the need for day care in industrial settings and the Welfare Council committee itself carried out a survey of day care needs in Jasper Place. Through these two small studies, the committee identified the need for a study of day care standards, a study of day care needs, improved education for day care workers, and more public education about the needs for day care.

A major success of the committee was co-sponsoring courses in Child Growth and Development with the Faculty of Extension at the University of Alberta in the fall of 1961. An area of the Council's interest, which had been seen as crucial from the very beginning of the Council, was the matter of proper standards of education and practice for social work in the province. Because of the adoption scandal and the subsequent distrust of social workers by the province, Alberta's social welfare services were not staffed by social workers. In fact, as late as 1955, there were only 22 professionally-trained social workers north of Red Deer, and these were in private agencies and the City of Edmonton. In addition, there were no social work training courses in the province. This was a matter of considerable concern to the Council. Thus, these first courses, developed with the blessing of the province, were considered an important breakthrough:

"There was a gradual change in relationships [with the provincial Welfare Department] which was most noticeable in 1959 when the Deputy Minister Miller and the Superintendent of Child Welfare, Charlie Hill, retired. Right after that, Duncan Rogers and Ray Hagen came to see me, which considering the history of relationships between the Council and the Welfare Department was quite an act for them.

Their purpose was to ask if there was any way we could help to develop training for their staff since before that time, by definition, a person would not be hired if they were a social worker. They felt that having a good heart and loving kids had fulfilled its day. Ray, who had only two years left in terms of his inheriting the Deputy Minister-ship, was very very intent on getting something changed in terms of education for staff.

It was as a result of this that we arranged through Doug Smith for the Continuing Education Department to establish a Certificate Welfare Training Course for staff members of the Welfare Department. This was very important, and it turned out to be the predecessor of the school in Calgary . . . . We developed a liaison with the School of Social Work at UBC and some of their people came to give specific courses. As a result of these courses, people were eligible for this Certificate.

We recognized that the Certificate was not a substitute for social work training. So, lo and behold, the Provincial Welfare Department was willing to send staff members to UBC on full pay to get their BSW. So I felt that in terms of the goal of establishing and developing social work standards of personnel and training, this was one of the things that was substantial." (Nicholls, April 17, 1990)

These first courses were taught by Professor A.J.B. Hough, a Board member of the Council as well as faculty member of the university, and were attended by over 100 staff members from children's services in Edmonton. The courses then became standard for several years under the auspices of the Faculty of Extension. Meanwhile a new committee, the Welfare Services Course Planning Committee, chaired by Merril McDonald of the Department of National Health and Welfare, worked on a brief which, in 1966, was presented to the Department of Education requesting the establishment of a two year welfare services course. The government accepted the recommendations of the brief and the first two-year social services technology course was set up at Nait in the fall of 1967.

While the education committees were carrying on, the committee involved with day care had continued with the original concerns. By early 1963, the committee's reports to the Board indicated that the research section of the Council should do a major study of day care.

One of the results of the Council's self-study had been an increased emphasis on high quality research. Since Gustave deCocq had been hired in 1956, he had been given several educational leaves to upgrade his education in social work, with particular concentration on research. Thus, as the sixties began, the Council had both the desire to do more research and the trained staff available. The Council Board agreed with the Day Care Committee's report, and recommended that the first stage of the study be done specifically in relation to the Creche given the uncertain future of that organization at the time:

We believe it is important for this community to have at least one high standard day care service facility able to incorporate elements of ongoing research in its work. It is logical that the Creche should be challenged to consider this role with the help of the Council. (Report of the Executive Committee to the Board of Directors on the Recommendations of the Day Care Committee, Jan. 30, 1963)

"As the work of the research committee began, however, it became clear that the members of the Board of the Creche were in the process of re-evaluating their own purpose and function in the light of thirty years of operation. Finally, in the spring of 1964, the Creche Directors dropped the bombshell: they were going to close the creche permanently. Bettie Hewes, President of the Council at the time, describes the problem:

. . . the Creche folded. It threatened to fold and then it folded . . . .

The Creche was for indigent women, women who had been abandoned. It was a private non-profit run by a Board and the Board members decided that their services were no longer needed based on the fact that more and more of the women who needed child care were women who appeared to have more means. That is, their stories ran 'Why, they come in cars!'. If times were such and the economy were such that these families could afford to drive cars, then surely they didn't need a subsidized child care!

So that was the setting for the gradual awakening in the good people of the community, the volunteers, and the voluntary agencies, that in fact, family life was different, that our mix in the city was different, and that we had to reorganize ourselves along different lines." (Hewes, Feb. 5, 1990)

Stewart Bishop, by this time working as Executive Director of the Council, describes how some of this reorganization began:

"What it [the reason for closure] really turned out to be was that the women [on the Board] who started the Creche actually ran it. In other words, they changed the babies and they looked after them. They didn't have staff. It was a volunteer effort, and they'd done it — one of them had done it for 34 years. No wonder they were burnt out! So they announced the Creche would close.

When I read this I went across to Norm Lansdowne, the Executive Director [of the Fund], and said 'What are you guys going to do about this? You've given them 30,000 bucks. How are you going to justify what they're saying?' Then when Tevie Miller [president of the Fund] phoned, I asked him, 'What are you going to do?'

He said 'it's what you're going to do, not me. You're going to do a study.' So Barbara Scott on our staff did the study and this was what lead to the recommendations that there should be a central creche, but also a series of centres in the suburbs. The city picked it up and then the Preventive Social Services funding came in, and it took off." (Bishop, March 7, 1990)

The Creche itself was immediately re-opened by an interim board put together by the Fund, Council, and City Welfare so that the children would have care. The Council developed an extensive Brief and delivered it to the City of Edmonton in March, 1966. The Brief covered the major concerns which the Council had been working on including improved standards and increased numbers of day care places. It also placed the responsibility squarely in the lap of the City Welfare Department:

In view of the critical need at the moment for licensed day care spaces, the Edmonton Welfare Council recommends and strongly urges:

That the City of Edmonton Welfare Department establish immediately a Day Care Section, with citizen representation, to assume

a) long-range responsibility, with the consultation and cooperation of the Edmonton Welfare Council, for the implementation of plans for the development of day care services in suburban and central areas of Edmonton in demonstrated need of such service; and

b) immediate responsibility for the establishment of a pilot day care service outside the central core of the city and offering a professionally-directed program of group care for children from 3 - 6 years of age and of supervised foster family day care for children under age three; . . . (Brief to the City of Edmonton on the Establishment of Day Care Services)

The Brief was accepted by the City, and then, as Stewart Bishop pointed out, the coincident development of the Preventive Social Services legislation allowed the day care services to expand almost immediately to begin filling the need.

The development of Preventive Social Services in the mid-sixties demonstrates the changing state of welfare services right across Canada. Books such as *The Vertical Mosaic* and Adams', *The Real Poverty Report* in Canada had begun to awaken the public to the reality of poverty in Canada. The Federal Government, often a minority government during this period, initiated several of its social security reforms, such as the Canadian and Quebec Pension Plans, Medicare, and the Canada Assistance Plan which provided for greater cost sharing of social services between federal and provincial governments (Wass, Address to the ESPC Annual Meeting, May 21, 1980). It was the Canada Assistance Plan which led to the Preventive Social Services legislation:

"When the Canada Assistance Plan came in, it had a major impact in shifting the responsibility for services from the private to the public sector. Duncan Rogers [Deputy Minister of Provincial Welfare Department] phoned me up and said 'I have ten million dollars I don't know what to do with. Can we plan something to prevent all these things from happening?'

There was Norman Lansdowne from the United Fund, myself from the Welfare Council, and the two counterparts from Calgary, and the head of the City Welfare Department, Keith Wass, and the head of the Calgary Department. We met for about a year. Duncan Rogers insisted that it had to be legislation and we insisted that it had to be community-based. The question was how do you get municipalities and communities to develop preventive services.

Prevention is really what I call outside the welfare system; that is, it has to happen before people need welfare. So it's education and any kind of preventive service, keeping people healthy, for example. Of course, day care was one of the major things that prevented people from going on assistance. So with the crisis at the Creche going on at the same time, this was a natural." (Bishop, March 7, 1990)

Thus, the development of day care services in Edmonton was a good example of what could be accomplished by private and public social welfare bodies working together when the timing and social climate were right. What is also interesting, however, is that the Council was not content to rest as the general concept of day care became more accepted. Even while the Day Care Planning Committee was doing its research for the Brief to the city, the Council was also participating in a group which was developing a pre-school Readiness Centre for children in the Norwood area.

This group, which included the National Council of Jewish Women, the Junior League, and the University of Alberta Departments of Educational Psychology and Elementary Education, was studying the possible advantages of school readiness training for "culturally deprived children". (Annual Report, 1966) Together, they developed Edmonton's first HeadStart program. Along with this Readiness Centre group as well as with others, the Council would continue into the seventies examining the need for specialized content and different forms of day care for disadvantaged children, deriving its basic information ultimately from the children and mothers themselves.

The Council's increasing use of research as a tool in its work showed up in many other projects during the sixties, particularly in the Youth Division. These included a survey of young people in north east Edmonton as to their leisure time needs and services and their values, ideals, and ethical beliefs. A major study of the juvenile court was presented in 1960, after which the Division worked very hard for the development of a Juvenile Court Committee which could advise on improvements. Marjorie Bowker, later a Juvenile Court judge, was one of the Council members who was a prime mover in this work. In addition, there were studies on delinquency, on facilities for emotionally disturbed and retarded children, and on adoption, as well as smaller studies on the need for family life education, community use of schools, child care institutions, and studies for the United Fund on a variety of child care institutions such as the evaluation of services provided by Boysdale Camp.

The study of north east Edmonton young people provided another opportunity for the Council to go to the people themselves for its information. It also demonstrated the manner in which the Council was able to involve several sectors of the community, including city officials, private recreation groups, university professors and their classes in the work.

The North East Community Council came to the Council for information and advice on problems relating to youth in their area, particularly concerns about fighting and the use of alcohol at teen dances. A formal request was made that a survey of the needs of and services for youth in the area be done, and the work began. A committee of representatives from the Youth Division and the North East Community Council began meeting, and after consultation with Dr. James from the Department of Sociology at the University of Alberta, the committee drew up a three phase study:

1. A survey of existing facilities, programs, and leadership of the organized leisure-time activities of youth.
2. An appraisal of facilities, programs, and leadership by (a) the young people themselves, and (b) by adult community leaders, e.g. teachers, clergy, community league volunteer leaders, scout leaders, etc. (c) and by the owners or managers of such public places as pool halls, restaurants, drug stores, barber shops, etc. This phase was envisaged to take place in the form of interviews with a sample of young people in the area and with selected community leaders. In this particular phase of the study, information would also be collected on what young people did in their leisure-time, their attitudes toward adults and toward community organizations.
3. Analysis of all the information and subsequent recommendations for action. (North East Edmonton Young People: A Study of their Leisure Time Needs and Services and their Values, Ideals, and Ethical Beliefs)

At the same time as the committee was developing its guidelines, a further request came from the Home and School Council of Edmonton requesting that the study also include some questions about values, ideals, and ethical beliefs. This was included in the study although with some caveats:

> The additional question as formulated in the resolution from the Edmonton Home and School Council was much less definable. As a matter of fact, it was not certain there was a problem. The fact was, however, that people were talking and acting as if there was a problem. Fears and concerns were expressed in phrases such as: 'young people of today have lost faith' (in a super-human power as well as lost faith in basic human values such as love, consideration, kindness, justice, etc.) and 'young people today have no ideals beyond their own personal ones of success and acquisition.' (Interim Report, p. 5)

The study was carried out by questionnaires administered by volunteers to groups which operated youth activities in the area in their own or others facilities. In addition, an interview schedule was developed and administered to 156 young people between the ages of 13 and 19 by university students from Dr. Hirabayashi's class in social psychology.

Again, despite the coding of responses on IBM cards, the job of collating all the material proved a large one for the predominantly volunteer workforce. However, the Interim Report was published by the end of 1961 with several tables indicating both the activities of youth and some of their attitudes. The findings of the Interim Report were used to support a request for an area director from the Parks and Recreation Department for the North-East area, and the Welfare Council began to bring together representatives of recreation organizations to examine the implications of this report.

The Youth Division was not only a research oriented Division. It was also involved in a variety of action projects particularly in its work with the Teen Council:

"David Critchley, who we hired to head the Youth Division, was an absolutely amazing person who generated a lot of enthusiasm and activity among young people. I still think that some of the things that happened in the Youth Services Division never happened anywhere else in Canada. They had, for instance, a city wide teen council that had a Youth Project Day and they planted 5000 trees down by Kinsmen Park. This was just one thing of very very active youth projects." (Nicholls, April 17, 1990)

The Teen Council, which had become the official youth section of the Division in 1960, carried out activities such as the annual Edmonton Youth Conference which dealt with major social issues as they related specifically to youth, worked with the City Parks and Recreation committee to develop a Teen Park, developed television programs, worked with the Allied Arts Council, and worked with the Alcoholism Foundation to develop a youth advisory committee to the Foundation.

Thus, the Youth Services Division was a major force in the work of the Council during the early sixties. However, in 1963, David Critchley left the Council. While replacements were found who were able to carry on the work of the Division itself, it seemed that with the departure of Critchley the problems of the relationship between the Council and its Division became more obvious. By 1966, there began to be many instances of disagreements over funds and priorities:

"As far as the Council itself, it [the Youth Services Division] produced an interesting problem. Because it had its own funding and its own committee in charge, and because it was a very powerful group, there was quite a debate as to what the Executive and the Board [of the Council] did and what the Executive of the Youth Services Division did.

. . . this debate between the two groups [went] on for ten years. I thought to myself 'there's something wrong here. It doesn't matter who is on the Board and who is on the Committee, they're fighting with each other. I happened to mention this to a woman who very cheerfully said 'Oh, a problem in group sovereignty.' . . .

It suddenly struck me that we had two groups making policy. So I said 'let's get the Executive of the Council and the Youth Services Division together. [We had a meeting] and John Patterson made an eloquent speech about why the Youth Division was very important. At one point somebody said to me, 'And what do you think of that, Stewart?' and to my horror, I hadn't been listening. I certainly got everyone's attention, unintentionally. I said 'I don't think any of the discussion we've had even for the last 10 years is relevant. What's really been happening is that we have two groups determining the policy of the Welfare Council and I think you guys have to decide if you're going to have two or one.' There was nothing more said about it until at some time later the Chairman of the Youth Services Division said that he thought we should merge the membership of the two groups into one." (Bishop, March 7, 1990)

Thus in 1966, it was agreed that the Youth Services Division would be absorbed into the Council and all the work would be done under the unified leadership. Since that time, the full Council has taken the responsibility, the kudos, and the complaints for all work with youth.

Chapter Eleven

A Motivated Council

While the Youth Services Division was busy with day care, delinquency, and the Teen Council, the "senior" section of the Council
was continuing work begun in the fifties with and on behalf of several
groups including seniors, immigrants, and the rehabilitation groups.

The study of seniors had been both a success — in its broad coverage
of seniors' issues and its extensive use of volunteers to do community
research — and a frustration — in respect to the difficulties the Council
had in finishing the complete report on the project. Dr. James, the
research associate from the university had university writing as the
priority in his work, and the Council staff had many many calls on
their time.

One of the major strengths of the Council, however, from the very
beginning was its ability to draw skilled, dedicated, and determined
individuals into its orbit:

> "There was a very strong contingent of volunteers in the com-
> munity. I must really emphasize that, because it was through them
> that both in Edmonton and Calgary, there was a a will to ensure
> that there were proper standards or services, proper accountability
> for services, that the needs of the community would be addressed."
> (Nicholls, Apr. 17, 1990)

Patricia Thom (Lobsinger) was one of those volunteers. She chaired
the Study Committee on Aging from the very beginning, 1956 through
1964, was involved in the study design, financing, and interviewing
in the early stages as well as in many of the offshoots of the report,
and chaired the volunteer editorial committee through weekly meetings
for a year in the '60s as they prepared the report for publication:

> "Bill Nicholls was head of the Council and he was much behind
> it [the study]. On the Council we had Doug Smith who was Dean
> of Arts, who was very central to it, and we had Bob James from

Sociology. They were of inestimable help to us. Aside from that it was volunteer work, totally. They were advisors and made expertise available to us to get going, but it was all ours. We worked very hard, and we had a good Board . . . ." (Interview, Patricia Thom, April 29, 1990)

The 269 page report, published in 1964, covered economic, health, recreation, and housing characteristics of seniors. In addition, it looked at attitudes concerning particular problem areas, problems of dependency, influences of church attendance and denomination, and influences of residence in particular neighbourhoods. In all, it presented one of the most comprehensive surveys of the elderly that has been done in Canada even today. Data from the study were used in many ways including providing information for the Housing for the Aged programme of the Provincial Department of Welfare, for the Provincial Municipal Committee on Homes for the Aged, and for the Council's submission to the Hall Commission on health care. It also provides a good example of the strength of the Council as a volunteer agency:

"It was always a good Council. That's one thought I have, that the Edmonton Welfare Council was a better Council — don't ask me why — than most of the committees like that I've been on since, and I've been on millions . . . . We didn't have any qualms about who we asked [to help]. I asked all sorts of people that probably now I'd feel a bit dumb about asking, like Doug Smith who was Dean of Arts, a lot of people who were [important] in the community, but I thought they'd be interested and they were . . . .

Things have become so stratified. Nowadays organizations just hire everything out. I don't see how anyone has any sense of learning or fulfillment in a project that way . . . . Ours was a really motivated Council." (Thom, April 29, 1990)

Certainly, some of the appeal of the Council to volunteers was the sense of learning and fulfillment that Patricia Thom mentions. Bill Nicholls suggests that a sense of personal responsibility and efficacy was another possible reason for that appeal:

"It really struck me the amount that people were prepared to devote in terms of their time and energy to the concerns around them, around the community. There was a lively volunteer community. It was always my feeling that people who were spending their time as volunteers should get credit for what it was that was being done because they earned it. So my approach to volunteers was that of indirect leadership, of assisting them, clarifying problems or strategies or whatever, but it was their responsibility. So they were very effectively involved in decision-making . . . ." (Nicholls, April 17, 1990)

Nicholls also suggests that the Council provided a place in the community for people who had that sense of community responsibility but no political forum through which to express it:

"The opposition in terms of social issues and social programs to what the government was doing was in the Council and the Council attracted the best people in terms of their sophistication and knowledge . . . . We were not involved politically, but in terms of a 'loyal opposition' stating the need for standards and the need for services properly set up for children and for young people and so on, this [the Council] was a constituency of people who were not strict adherents of the government party. I think that people who were concerned about these things felt that the Council was a stable organization that could deliver things that they felt related to their interests, their citizen and political interests. It was very distinctly a nucleus of opposing views." (Nicholls, April 17, 1990)

Thus the volunteers had the rewards, in the personal sphere, of learning and fulfillment, and the reward, in a more public sphere, of having some observable influence on decisions made about the social issues and social programs of their community.

Certainly, the volunteers who worked on the varied issues of the rehabilitation committee through the sixties had a strong commitment to their work, and ultimately, were able to see real achievements.

As the sixties began, there were three main local groups involved in some aspect of rehabilitation for the disabled: the Rehabilitation Society, a direct service agency for the physically and mentally disabled; the Rehabilitation Study Group, a group of people primarily connected to rehabilitative service agencies who met to exchange information and ideas; and the Standing Committee on Rehabilitation, a Council committee established for study, planning and action on rehabilitation needs. These groups were concerned about duplication of their efforts, duplication of personnel, and about their general efficacy in the community. Several possible ways of amalgamating were examined and the most favoured was to form a Rehabilitation Division of the Council, analogous to the Youth Division.

Considerable study was devoted to this end, including drawing up a constitution for the Division. However, the main stumbling block was the matter of the funding for a separate Division with its own staff and research capability. It was also noted that in this case there was a Provincial Co-ordinator for Rehabilitation, hired under a Federal-Provincial cost-sharing program, who would be taking the responsibility for co-ordination of activities. Thus, in 1961, it was decided that there were insufficient funds to set up a separate Division; however, the Council would continue to deal with rehabilitation through committees studying specific issues. The Rehabilitation Study Group disbanded and sent its concerns to the Council.

One of the first issues to be explored was the question of transportation for the disabled. A report was put together by the Council surveying the existing transportation facilities. It was found that there were five agencies in the city owning altogether ten small vehicles and two larger buses. In addition, the Central Volunteer Bureau provided volunteer drivers to transport people to and from the six other major services for the disabled which had no transportation capacity. The Council decided that a meeting of all of these organizations was in order to determine what the level of satisfaction was with the existing system, and whether the organizations would consider pooling their resources in a single unified system.

Meetings were held through the fall of 1962 and winter of 1963 until a meeting, May 28, 1963, chaired by Keith Wass, member of the Council Board and Director of the City Welfare Department. At this meeting, the organizations involved finally agreed that a co-ordinated system might be more beneficial. However, it was felt that none of the agencies currently transporting their own clientele should take on the task of running the co-ordinated system. Thus, it was agreed that the Council should approach the Alberta Council for Crippled Children and Adults to suggest their setting up such a system. Financing would, it was hoped, come from the Easter Seals, the United Fund, from municipal and provincial governments, and from fees for service.

For some time, the Alberta Council for Crippled Children and Adults followed up on the Transportation Study. However, not all of the organizations which already had transportation wanted an integrated system. A stalemate was reached and the problem handed back to the

Council. At the same time, the Cerebral Palsy Association came to the Council asking for support of its request to the United Community Fund for "additional funds to put a vehicle on the road for the transportation of handicapped persons to and from treatment centres." (Minutes, Executive Committee, October 25, 1965) The Council supported this request, and also supported the continuation of efforts to develop a co-ordinated system. Mrs. Edna Laforge, a Council Board member and member of the Multiple Sclerosis Society, was appointed to head the Council committee. The committee's work was hampered, but never halted, by inter-agency tensions:

Although there was obvious inter-agency tension throughout the meeting, discussion was good. Many diversified points of view were expressed, and we are confident this tension was dissipated somewhat and a better inter-agency working relationship established.

It would appear to be very important that the agency setting up the coordinated transportation system should impartially represent the various agencies needing the services. (Memorandum, Edna LaForge to Board of Directors, 1966)

When a totally co-ordinated system could not be agreed on, this committee's interim plan was to approach the Fund and the Alberta Council for Crippled Children and Adults to set up a pilot project to provide transportation for those agencies which did not already have transportation. After considerable work, negotiation, and some compromise, the various parties agreed in March 1966 that the Cerebral Palsy Association would operate an Edmonton Handi-Bus pilot project for eighteen months. A management committee was set up for the project, and problems not able to be solved by that committee would be referred first to the Cerebral Palsy Association Board of Directors, and then, if necessary, to the Edmonton Welfare Council. An Evaluation Committee, headed by Edna LaForge, was set up with members from the Fund, the Council, and the public.

The pilot project ended December 1967, and the Evaluation Report was presented to the Council Board in March of '68. The chief recommendations were that a co-ordinated service be continued and expanded, but that to guard the service's impartiality, a new independent agency should be set up to manage it:

a) An independent agency, financed by the United Community Fund, would remove any doubt of the Handi-Buses operation being connected financially with a disease entity association.
b) An independent Board of Directors would not be influenced by any participating agency.
c) All persons using the service would receive like treatment with regard to subsidization by the community. (Report of the Evaluation Committee, Edmonton Handi-Buses, February 1968)

The Council, and then the United Community Fund, accepted the recommendations of the Evaluation Committee; a separate Edmonton Handi-Bus Association was formed and continued the service until the City of Edmonton took over the service and renamed it the Disabled Adults Transit System (DATS).

Another issue of importance in rehabilitation was the issue of assessment services for the disabled. This issue arose when the Edmonton Epilepsy Association approached the United Community Fund for money for a staff social worker. The Fund Admissions and Evaluations Committee referred this request to the Council for study. Again, a volunteer committee, chaired by Dr. Mintz, was formed, and the Council proceeded to investigate, more generally, the availability of counselling services for the disabled. The results of this study led the Council to the position that provincial assessment teams, able to assess the total needs of a disabled person, were the first priority.

A province-wide commiittee of representatives from the Edmonton Welfare Council, the Calgary Social Planning Council, the Alberta Council for Crippled Children and Adults, and the Canadian Medical Association, Alberta Division, was formed in 1964 and presented a brief to the provincial government in 1966. The philosophy of team assessment was stated clearly in the brief. It was intended to provide a service which would look at all aspects of a person and develop a thorough plan which included use of community resources as well as specific agency resources:

Integrated assessment, as envisaged by our committee, involves all appropriate professional disciplines necessary for the complete evaluation of the handicapped person. Only in this way can a comprehensive report of the whole person be obtained. Further, this assessment does not constitute an end in itself. It is no more than the preliminary requirement for prescription of a rehabilitation program which will realize the maximum potential of the individual. The assessment services must therefore be able to call upon the resources of physicians and surgeons of all specialties, therapists, psychologists, social workers, vocational counsellors, work assessment personnel, and placement officers. (Brief on Team Assessment To The Government Of The Province of Alberta, August 1966.)

At first, the government, through the Department of Health, responded unenthusiastically to the report. However, the Council Board continued to promote the idea, and after receiving some support from the Deputy Minister of Public Welfare, Duncan Rogers, they went back to the Department of Health to once again urge the importance of the concept. In September 1968, a provincial pilot study program was begun in Edmonton at the Glenrose Hospital.

This program had an Advisory Committee of representatives from the original group which presented the Brief plus a representative from Manpower and from the Vocational Education Department. This Advisory Committee met with a standing committee of the medical staff of the Glenrose set up for the program. Mrs. Enid Crockett, one of the Council's representatives on the Advisory Committee, reported that unfortunately the integration of community people with the medical people was not proceeding easily:

1) The medical facilities offered to the patient are excellent and under Dr. Bhala's capable direction the assessments are very thorough.
2) The Team is heavily medically oriented and there appears to be little or no point in lay members being on the committee. Lay members have stated both at the meetings and privately that attendance at the meetings is a waste of time for them as far as any constructive participation in the work of the Team is concerned. (Report re Disability Team Assessment, February 1969)

In addition to the problem of the functioning of the team, it was noted that there were some difficulties in getting the service to work in a streamlined manner. However, these were secondary. In response to Mrs. Crockett's assessment, the Council Board noted that "the success of the disability team assessment depended primarily on it being a community service" (Board of Directors Minutes, February 3, 1989). If the team was to only involve medical assessments, it would not be providing the comprehensive community service envisaged.

There were many other important projects which the Council worked on during the sixties. A detailed inventory of community services was carried out for the United Community Fund with one staff person hired soley for this purpose. In addition, the Council became more involved in responding to matters of physical planning, including the City of Edmonton's Parks and Recreation Master Plan, the use of the river valley, and the need for public housing to be developed by the city. The Council also continued to be involved with seniors. Using information from the major study, a smaller study was done of the need for Meals on Wheels. This program was then implemented by the Victorian Order of Nurses (VON) with the assistance of the Council.

There was also activity in the area of assisting immigrants. The Council had worked with refugee organizations since World War, and this had become a significant part of its work after the Hungarian revolution in 1956. Council's interest continued through the sixties predominantly by promoting human rights and multi-culturalism by means such as holding a two-day conference in June 1963, "Insights into Cultural Differences". In addition, Welfare Information Service found itself making many referrals for new immigrants.

After the "Prague Spring" of 1968, the refugee issue assumed new urgency and the Council initiated a special information service staffed by a Czech immigrant and funded by the United Community Fund. This apparently straight-forward information-giving project had some unexpected aspects:

"Because there was a very small Czech community here, we set up a Czech Information Centre as a temporary part of the Council, and hired one of the newly arrived refugees, Sasha, to run it. She had good English and knew a lot about government. She was very good. There was a steady stream of Czech refugees coming in. We tried to get them matched up with people in the community with some understanding of the language who could help them with housing and clothing, training, English, and jobs. It wouldn't have been so difficult if it had been, say, Ukrainian, but because the existing core of Czechs was so small, it was thought that we had to do something. The Council was the logical place for such a short-term service.

One day, I became aware that there was some odd activity out there [in the main office space] and Sasha was anxious. A day or so went by, and there seemed to be some more activity [that was unusual] so I talked to her. She finally admitted that there were two cops, RCMP, hovering, trying to get information out of her about the people she was dealing with.

When they came back again, I asked them to come in and sit down. I can remember saying, 'Do you always travel in twos, like nuns?' Then I said, 'you know there's a Director here, and a Board of Directors who run this show, and Sasha works for us. If you've got something to say, you come to us. But you're not going to threaten someone around here.' So they got a little nicer." (Hewes, February 5, 1990)

Thus, the first eight years of the sixties was a time of tremendous activity on the part of the Council, working on a wide variety of issues, many of them issues on which the Council had begun to work in the fifties, or as with day care, even in the forties. At the same time, however, the Council was beginning to move into some less traditional areas and was beginning to develop some new approaches in its work.

Chapter Twelve

New Voices

Concern about unemployment and transiency was an issue, like the concerns for seniors, for heath services, and for rehabilitation, which had been with the Council since the fifties. But the developments in the work with transients in the sixties help delineate the way Council was changing both in attitudes and style of work. At the beginning of the sixties, the Council was primarily speaking with other agencies and acting as a voice for transients. By 1969, one of the voices of the Council was the voice of the transients themselves.

During the fifties, much of the concern about transients had centered around the lack of even the most basic facilities such as sufficient beds for the unemployed men who were arriving in the city. This shortage of beds had been alleviated somewhat by the provision of additional hostel facilities through the Salvation Army, the Provincial Hostel, and some private accommodation made available to men on a nightly basis. As the sixties began, however, unemployment seemed to be increasing and bringing with it additional problems.

In November 1960, the Council called a meeting of interested agencies to pool their information and resources. The list of agencies that participated in that meeting was a long one, although the Provincial Hostel, an invitee, was noticeably absent:

> Edmonton Family Service Bureau, City Welfare Department, Beverly Welfare Department, Provincial Welfare Department, Salvation Army, Marian Centre, YWCA, Multiple Sclerosis Society, National Employment Service, the Anglican Social Service Council, Jewish Welfare Society and All People's Mission. (Unemployment and Related Problems in Edmonton: A Review of the Present Situation with Recommendations for Action, Nov. 1960)

The information from these agencies confirmed that unemployment and transiency were on the rise. The National Employment Service reported 9750 unplaced applicants compared to 8312 the year before; the Marian Centre reported providing 200 more meals per day than had been provided during the same period in 1959; All People's Mission reported a 50 per cent increase in requests for clothing. The meeting concluded with a motion that the Council "take steps to have the Provincial Government re-evaluate its present programme with regard to single transients". (Management Committee Report on Social Welfare Services Related to Unemployment, Nov. 30, 1960) The meeting also asked that the Council consider the other problems raised at the meeting and attempt to co-ordinate any action on those problems.

In fact, many problems had been raised. These included such matters as the fact that the provincial government services only provided two meals per day for the single male transient; that provision of clothing was done by voluntary agencies in an unco-ordinated fashion at best; that there were no routine medical examinations for transients; that there was no provision for the leisure-time of the homeless person who was not allowed to stay in the hostels during the day-time hours. It was also noted that the position of the female transient was even less enviable than that of the male: "Many persons are of the opinion . . . that the present practice of housing single female transients in hotels (usually third rate) encourages efforts to solve their problems by prostitution." (Management Committee Report, Nov. 30, 1960)

In response to the meeting and its suggestions, the Council set up a continuing committee to spearhead work on the various problems. The first step was to send information on the unemployment situation in Edmonton to the Canadian Welfare Council which was preparing a Brief for the Senate Committee on Unemployment. Also out of this concern with transients, as well as concurrent projects, the Council staff developed its submission to Justice Emmett Hall's Royal Commission on Health. This submission, "Medical Care and Hospital Services for the Indigent and Medically Indigent", raised issues such as the connection between ill health and welfare need; the problems of the indigent in paying for drugs, diets, or appliances; the need for social service departments at all hospitals; the need for dental care for the poor; and the health needs of seniors.

In terms of actually alleviating the day-to-day problems of the transients, the committee, at first, felt some discouragement because of the national scope of the problem. However, in early 1962, they were able to make practical progress on the specific problem of leisure time.

All People's Mission, which was already providing clothing for transients, had bought a building, known as the Old Polish Hall, and offered it for a day centre. Working with the Mission, the committee developed a plan for the centre which was subsequently accepted by the United Community Fund for funding.

The Centre was established, and at first, there seemed to be some rivalry between it and the Marian Centre as to which agency should be providing what rehabilitation services. However, it was soon acknowledged that there were enough unemployed and transient men on the streets to warrant both services operating, and the Day Centre was proclaimed a success:

> You may remember that just about a year ago we reported on the results of a citizens' committee investigating the best means of offering daytime shelter and rehabilitation to homeless unemployed men in our community. This committee was brought together by the Council after several months of research and study. They continued to operate under the aegis of the Council until a duly registered organization, the Edmonton Day Centre, was formed to translate their plan into action. The Council has continued support of the Day Centre throughout the year with both staff and volunteer assistance and we are most pleased to observe the high standards of the resulting service which is now available. (Annual Report, 1963)

The work of this committee on unemployment followed the classical Council method: bring together the concerned agencies; identify and analyze problems; prepare information and recommendations for appropriate authorities such as government; provide staff and consultation to assist local groups or agencies to develop a service to fill particular identified gaps. But with the new emphasis on community development as a way of working, and with a new understanding of its own role, the Council's work with transients began to take other forms as well. To look at these new ways of working, it is necessary to look at some of the new issues with which the Council was becoming involved.

One of the most significant developments in Council work during the sixties was its growing concern with the relationship between physical planning and social planning. Beginning with its self-study, the Council had increasingly defined its role as a planning role. At first, this had been seen as primarily social welfare planning although there had been study of the problems of housing conducted by the Health Division as early as the forties, and the Council had presented a brief to the Royal Commission on Metropolitan Planning in 1954. But any compartmentalization of categories of planning was, in the sixties, gradually seen as artificial:

"Social planning is the same as any other kind of planning. There isn't anything except people. Why we differentiate between social planning and physical planning I really don't know because 'people is all there is'. And so everything is social planning as far as I'm concerned. Unfortunately a lot of planning that occurs is not planning but is rearranging. That's not bad, we need to rearrange from time to time, and I suppose it's all right to call that planning. But planning for me has got to be moving out to reform, to 're-form' something, and to put it together and do it differently, hopefully to improve the human condition." (Hewes, February 5, 1990)

Alan Affleck, as Chairman of the Activities Committee of the Council, was one of the first to act on this expanding view of social planning:

". . . I became more and more convinced about the role of the community . . . so I went to a meeting of the Community Planning Association of Canada because they were dealing with topics such as space to play, school yards, and the river valley. I spoke up a couple of times and ended up being invited to go on the executive of the Edmonton Branch. It was a group of laymen interested in physical planning. Subsequently when I was on the Board [of the Council] I was President of the Community Planning Association and therefore I worked for co-operation between those two . . . .

We held a joint meeting about the river valley. What could we do to protect it? What could we do to utilize it in an intelligent way? . . ." (Alan Affleck, March 7, 1990)

This meeting was held in November 1962 and could be said to mark the real beginning of the Council's involvement with the physical elements of planning as they related to people. As it moved into 1963, the Council became thoroughly involved with the City of Edmonton as well as the Community Planning Association in work on physical planning, especially urban renewal.

Urban renewal had come somewhat later to Edmonton than to other parts of the country, but in 1962 the city signed an agreement with Central Mortgage and Housing to undertake an urban renewal study of certain inner city neighbourhoods. An Urban Renewal Division of the City Planning Department was created, and from the beginning, the staff of this new section worked closely with staff from the Edmonton Welfare Council:

Firstly, in consultation on the overall study; secondly, in technical consultation on the social survey, the second phase of this study; and thirdly, in consultation on the process of urban renewal. (Annual Report, 1963)

Along with the City and the Community Planning Association, the Council sponsored a series of neighbourhood "grass-roots" meetings. Gus deCocq, Acting Director in 1963 after Bill Nicholls had left the Council, described the purpose of these meetings in his report to the Board:

I participated in the first of a series of 'grass roots' meetings in the McCauley district. This was held on the assumption that 1) the residents of an area that might be affected by Urban Renewal must have a say in any changes that are going to take place; and that 2) information about the residents and their hopes, desires, problems and aspirations will prove extremely useful in the formulation of a plan that will suit the neighborhood. This first meeting proved our assumptions entirely valid. (November 28, 1963)

The first study on which the Urban Renewal Division and the Edmonton Welfare Council collaborated "identified the Boyle Street Area as the 'poorest district which contains many characteristics associated [with] skid row' (A Study of Collaborative Effort Between Two Formal Organizations, p. 4). Subsequent efforts of the Urban Renewal Division and the Edmonton Welfare Council to collaborate in the Boyle Street Area were largely stymied at a formal level by organizations of the senior levels of government such as the Alberta Housing and Urban Renewal Committee and Canada Mortgage and Housing. Both of these organizations determined that any studies must be carried out by planning professionals supervised by the municipal organizations rather than collaboratively, by physical and social planners and volunteers, despite the recommendations by the Urban Renewal chief planner. Ultimately, there was little effect of urban renewal in Edmonton, with or without collaboration, since it was discredited as an approach across Canada before there were major changes made in the landscape of Edmonton's skid row.

Nevertheless, the informal collaboration that took place between Urban Renewal and the Council brought the Council more immediately into contact with the people of the Boyle Street area, many of whom were the unemployed transients with whom their previous agency work had been concerned. Such contact made the issues of unemployment and housing, particularly in Boyle Street, appear critical, although the urban renewal survey, done by the senior government's "professional" planning approach, had managed to ignore these transients and their problems:

The transient population of the area which is substantial and characteristic of one part of the area was ignored for two reasons. First, a significant number of the 'skid row' element were assumed to possess pathological characteristics that the interview schedule was not prepared to handle appropriately. Second, the Civic Centre Urban Renewal Scheme proposals would concern themselves, first and foremost, with the possible displacement of the permanent population. (Urban Renewal Report)

Neither the Senior Planner of the Urban Renewal Division (who subsequently resigned) nor Stewart Bishop, Executive Director of the Welfare Council beginning in 1964, were happy with this approach, which would result simply in the movement of transients to areas adjacent to the proposed urban renewal area.

At the same time as the Council was surveying the Boyle Street area with Urban Renewal, they were also beginning to work with various Indian and Metis organizations. During the late fifties, there had been occasional requests by native organizations for the assistance of the Council, but these had been refused on the basis of lack of staff and other resources. In 1960, however, the Council began work in this area. The question of working with the native community was first raised in the Youth Division because of reports that Indian and Eskimo youth were being denied hotel accommodation when visiting relatives at the Camsell hospital. An Indian and Metis Study Committee, chaired by Gerry Amerongen, was set up in November 1960 and reported in March 1962.

The report stressed the variety and uniqueness of the problems facing the urban native:

The Indians and Metis have been reared with a basically different cultural heritage than ours. His way of life, (to describe the archetype) places different emphases on time, savings, sharing, work habits, and in general his orientation to nature. His was the way of adjusting to nature, rather than in shaping nature. His essence of life was found in being and not in becoming . . . .

The Indians and Metis who come to Edmonton . . . are essentially rural. Therefore, they have all of the adjustment problems that confront rurally-oriented peoples as they face urban living.

And most important of all the Indians and Metis, on the whole, are members in our society of the lower socio-economic class, in fact, the lower-lower. All of the tremendous problems of adjusting successfully to a western urban society are compounded by the problems of the lower-lower class. These are characterized in poor education, poor housing, little skills for occupations, little aspirations to achieve, poor health, apathy and depression. (Report of the Indian and Metis Study Committee, March 5, 1962)

The report made eight recommendations to the Board of the Council. These included recommendations about the need for appropriate foster and adoptive homes for native children, for examination of negative stereotypes in school text books, for public education, and for anti-discrimination legislation. More immediately, the report recommended that the Council actively support a committee already working on the creation of a native friendship centre:

The committee recommends that the Board of the Council of Community Services participate in the development of a friendship centre in Edmonton, similar to that which has been developed in Winnipeg.
a) It would act as a meeting place for people of Indian and Eskimo background.
b) It would act as a centre for recreation, informal education and leadership training for the Indian people.
c) It would act as a referral centre, where people of Native background needing special services could be referred to appropriate services and organizations in the community.

This centre, through its services would help the people of Indian and Eskimo background bridge the gulf between their culture and western urban culture. (Report of the Indian and Metis Study Committee, March 5, 1962)

With Council staff assistance and consultation, the Native Friendship Centre was established. Again, while working specifically with natives was new to the Council, the pattern of work — study an issue, then assist development of the gap-filling agency — was familiar.

Thus, in the mid-sixties, the Council was following several separate threads — unemployment and transiency, urban renewal, urban native problems — into the maze of community need which was Boyle Street. At the same time, the Council was beginning to consider community development and social action as possible planning tools. These new problem areas seemed to demand a new kind of work.

The provincial government of Alberta was, itself, being swept into community development during the early sixties, and had appointed Jim Whitford as a Community Development Officer to work with native people. These activities were primarily directed toward rural areas. The Council began to investigate the desirability of using community development as a technique in the urban centres. The staff met with Whitford several times in 1964 and '65 and invited him to speak to meetings of Council members and Board about community development and native problems. The Council also began to negotiate with the province for a community development worker to be attached to the Council to work with urban natives. The province was not prepared to pay for a Council community development worker, but did place a provincial worker in the urban setting.

For the Council, this was not sufficient. From the 1961 Annual Meeting with its "New Directions in Determining Community Change" theme, the staff and Board had both been looking at community development and social action. Stewart Bishop, hired as Executive Director in 1964 to follow Bill Nicholls, was deeply involved in the urban renewal work and the notion of community planning, and saw a need for a more action-oriented Council. Bettie Hewes, hired in 1967 to replace Barbara Scott, the previous research director, relates that her hiring was a move towards that social action approach:

"I went to work at the Mental Health Association [CMHA] and found myself very quickly into social action activity because services for the mentally ill in Alberta were terrible. We got immediately involved . . . in changing attitudes, in changing legislation and programs for the mentally ill. It was terribly

122

difficult, but highly successful, astonishingly successful. We had everybody in the province mobilized to yell and scream at the government about the circumstances, and they [the government] did, in fact, do a lot of looking and seeing, and there were some remarkable changes.

The Council, in the meantime, had Stewart Bishop as their Director. Stewart, I think, recognized that he needed some social action components in the Council, and he and others came after me and hired me . . . They had seen this agency, CMHA, really take off in social action and force some change and they wanted to add that dimension [to the Council]." (Hewes, February 5, 1990)

The hiring of Hewes as a planner with some responsibility for social action coincided with another rewriting of Council Objects and another change of name, this time to the Edmonton Social Planning Council. Louis D. Hyndman, President of the Council for 1966, described the reasons for that change in his President's Report:

. . . we are presenting to you a new name and a new constitution designed to develop an organization responsive to present and future community needs and capable of developing plans to meet them . . . .

While we are still involved in collaborating with agencies and groups of agencies around city-wide problems and concerns we are becoming increasingly convinced that the most outstanding deficiency in our pattern of welfare services is their lack of availability. This does not simply mean that we need more services than we now have. It does mean that all services are not equally available in all communities and neighbourhoods in our city. This realization has been forced upon us primarily by the concentration of interest in the Boyle Street area . . . . (Annual Report, 1966)

The new set of objects simplified the language of the 1961 objects, and more important, moved the focus of the Council squarely onto research and planning in relation to community problems and needs. It also put a new emphasis on the techniques of planning:

The primary objects of the Council shall be research into, and development of plans and proposals to fulfill the social needs of the citizens of the City of Edmonton and to define the techniques by which these plans and proposals may be implemented . . . .

In addition, the new Constitution made a dramatic change in eligibility for membership. Since 1940, the majority of members had been agency members who appointed delegates. As the Council moved closer to the view of itself as an organization of the community rather than of agencies, it revised its membership provisions to allow more and more individual members. In 1967, the provisions for agency members were abolished. All memberships would be individual. Over the years, there had been much discussion within the Council of the difficulties of creating a clear role and meaningful membership among delegates, so the move to individual membership was, in part, a recognition of this difficulty. It was also, however, a clear demonstration of the Council's growing emphasis on democratic and community values.

These changes also coincided with the merging of the Youth Services Division with the Senior Council, and this resulted in some substantial changes on the Board. Several members of the 1966 Youth Services Executive Committee, who were also involved in the university and the growing campus activism, became Board Members in 1967, among them Russell Kempton, Charles Hynam, and Gerry Wright. This was a particularly active and articulate group who brought with them new ideas about how things should be done.

Thus, by the end of 1967, the Social Planning Council had a constitution and staff with a community development/social action outlook, and a Board with several members committed to an activist Council which could shake up the status quo:

"The Council, up until the sixties, had been doing its work in a very normal fashion where the philosophy for social change was to make friends with the Deputy Minister and try to influence the Minister. You didn't really ever talk to the Minister himself. As you know, the young people in the sixties took exception to this kind of kowtowing acceptance of authority. So the explosion against authority took place and the Council played its role by really upsetting the whole 'old' Board of the time. There was too much structural change, too much behavioural change in the way the meetings were handled, [too much change in] the physical arrangement of the room where we met because we got rid of the Board table. People sat on benches or on the floor. These were all things to make a break with traditional patterns of behaviour and thinking." (Interview, Gerry Wright, February 8, 1990)

With the intent to make a break with traditional patterns and a background of work with transients, urban renewal, and urban Indians, the next moves of the Council to work directly with "the people" and to obtain its information "from the street" not other agencies were not surprising. In 1968, the Board of Directors of the Council, under President George Levine, decided that they should have their own community development worker in Boyle Street, and hired Lynn Hannley, as a "detached worker":

"My involvement with the Council [started] through the City because I was working for the City Parks and Recreation, doing recreational organizing in the inner city. A lot of the people I knew were involved with the Council, and offered me the job. Primarily, my job was to do inner city organizing with groups of people. I worked mostly from the old urban renewal office, and worked also with the guys on the street who organized a restaurant. Marc [Father Marc Barrier] and Ben Coutrel were involved in organizing it and I was helping them out . . . . The restaurant wasn't a Council project. It sort of became attached through the detached worker . . . . So I was all over on the street working with kids and transient men primarily." (Interview, Lynn Hannley, March 7, 1990)

In hiring their own community development worker, the Council had created a position which "provide[d] a direct contact between the Council and 'client groups' especially in Boyle Street area. It has added a new note of realism and urgency to the deliberations of Council" (Annual Report, 1968). That position, or rather the person in it, brought to the Council a whole network of people and projects which were already working directly with people on the skids, but who could use the support of the kind done by the Council. Thus, people like Father Marc Barrier, an Oblate Father who was working very closely with the skid row men, came to be an integral part of a Social Planning Council "extended family" of staff. George McDermott, the Metis president of the Native Brotherhood Society, was also one of the working network that developed around the detached worker.

The direct contact with the client, the note of realism and urgency of the work in Boyle Street, and the voices of this new group of workers, quickly permeated the thinking of the overall Council:

"The thinking of the Board had changed. They had begun to perceive the immense social problems that were developing in our community and the incapacity of individual agencies to meet and deal with those problems, the incapacity of individual agencies to collaborate to deal with them, and the incapacity to change. Perhaps they [the agencies] didn't need to change, they stayed with their own constituency.

But the Council saw some other things looming on the horizon and believed that we needed to do things differently; that is, we needed a different process and we needed a different content . . . . The tried and true methods were not working and were not going to be working. So we began to work in different ways. . . . The major change was a subtle but very definite acknowledgment that people knew what they needed. What we wanted was an agent that would free them up and give them the resources and create the environment where they would take control for themselves.

That knowledge was there. We weren't always able to actualize it, but it was there. It would slip away and we'd get fearful, then we'd reorganize ourselves and gather together, and we'd be okay again. It was not easy. The Council itself came under tremendous threat from people who had been our lifetime supporters." (Hewes, Feb. 5, 1990)

Thus, as the Council moved ahead in the last two years of the sixties, it had a Board, staff, and associates who were all prepared for planning in less traditional ways and for deriving their information from less traditional sources.

Chapter Thirteen

The Possible is Irrelevant

One of the important features of the Social Planning Council during the late sixties and early seventies was the web of human connections which grew, and in turn, created other connections. By 1968, there was a wave of egalitarianism sweeping North America. Within the Council, this egalitarianism expressed itself in two particular ways: first, the Council asserted that the voice of the poor, the people with the problems, was equal in value (perhaps greater than equal) to the voices of the professionals, the agencies, the academics. This led to a major emphasis in working at the grassroots.

Second, the Council also asserted, in its behaviour if not formally, that all workers were equal. Thus, although formal distinctions were maintained, in practice, the volunteer, the Board member, the paid Council worker, and the paid worker of other organizations were seen as "equal" workers in Council projects. Their contributions were accepted with equal enthusiasm. Many volunteers and some Board members worked virtually full-time and were, in all characteristics except salary, staff of the Council. In turn, individuals who joined this working web of the Council's brought with them their own set of contacts, projects, and enthusiasms as Lynn Hannley describes:

"What happened was that I had worked for the province in the summer of '67, prior to working for the city. I was organizing the preschool and I had a drop-in — a settlement house basically — for teens. When the summer was over, there was still a need for the teen [project]. There was still a need for the preschool too, but that was more of a summer programme. A lot of the people in the inner city were Native or Italian immigrants. So that's how the contact was made with the people for the Native Brotherhood — through their kids. They were either my contacts or Marc's contacts.

We continued working on the teen centre and some teens had actually made presentations to City Council about getting a Teen Centre before I was working for the Council . . . . The connection with the transient men came from working with the city and there was an expanded connection with Natives through Marc whose parish was the Native community and the transients. We basically worked, he and I, on organizing the Native Brotherhood. When I went to work for the Council — when they took me — they took my baggage with me." (Hannley, March 7, 1990)

At the same time, Rev. David Crawley was hired by Rev. Ronald Shepherd, at All Saints Cathedral, to work in the inner city. Rev. Shepherd had been a member of the Council's Board of Directors, and as he retired from the Board, David Crawley was elected. He brought with him involvement with another set of young people:

"It was the summer of 1968 and there was some talk about a youth centre. I went away on holidays in July, down east, and stopped in Winnipeg on my way back. There was a letter there from someone I'd never heard of, saying that a group of young people had gone to see Dean Shepherd at the Cathedral and he had agreed that there could be a youth drop-in centre in the Church hall. So I went on home and Ron Shepherd left on his holidays the next day. Middle Earth hadn't opened yet, but they'd begun to set it up. So there I was. . . ." (Interview, David Crawley, March 19, 1990)

Thus, for the summer of 1968, Middle Earth, the teen centre, operated in All Saints Cathedral Church hall. But from the beginning, this had been seen as a temporary measure, for the summer only, and for the most part, had not included the teens from the Boyle Street Area. The needs of these two groups merged in Council discussions, and with the Council Board as backup, the young people set up a meeting with the Mayor to present a proposal for establishing a permanent teen centre in the downtown area. The Social Planning Council wrote August 19, 1968, to Mayor Dantzer of their support for a youth-directed centre:

It is a fundamental principle of this total concept that the young people themselves must accept the responsibility of making all decisions in respect to the operation of such a centre. These decisions would include rules of operation, personnel, program content, finances, use of volunteers as counsellors, teachers and resource persons. (Report to His Worship Mayor Vincent Dantzer and Members of City Council regarding a Downtown Teen Centre.)

The Council offered to take on the administrative tasks associated with the proposed centre, under the direction of the youth organization.

This was a period when the "hippie" movement, with its symbols of peace signs, long hair, drugs, and the hitchhiker's thumb, was at the centre of public controversy, with citizens lining up, pro or con. The Council's support of a teen centre was not approved of by everyone. City Council, however, reacted favourably to the Teen Centre presentation, and promised to work with the teens and the Council to set up such a centre. The police, on the other hand, were not at all enthusiastic about having a place where youth would congregate. Two days before the All Saints Middle Earth Centre was scheduled to close, the municipal police and RCMP officers, with stocking masks hiding their faces, raided the centre, thus raising the tension around the whole issue of a downtown teen centre.

The Council continued to support the teens. Delegations of teens frequently made presentations to Council Board meetings and to members of the Civic Administration. The problem seemed to be to find an appropriate building, but the process dragged on:

"We did a lot of lobbying with the city, basically Vince Dantzer was the one who pushed it through. He was mayor at the time. And out of that we got a building, ... It took a long time to set it up, a year or so." (Crawley, March 19, 1990)

It was, in fact, the fall of 1969, before the city found a building, renovations were conducted, and Ed Delong was hired for the single staff position of "Enhancer". The Centre survived for slightly over a year with inconclusive results. A wide variety of activities for teens took place there, from crafts to counselling, to just "hanging out". On the other hand, regular visits by the police along with conflicts between the different groups of teens within the centre made it less successful than had been hoped. Rev. Crawley felt that part of the problem with the Centre was that it came too late:

"It was right at the end of the hippie era. The hippie movement, as such, in its original sort of pure idealism, vanished about 1967 in March when it went into Time magazine. But the spill-over was still there for a couple of years. There were substantial numbers of kids on the move the summer of '68, kids from out of town. A lot of the kids who hung around downtown were local kids though — that was just the thing to do. But there was a small percentage of them that was socially and emotionally dispossessed . . . .

Basically the downtown youth centre attempted to be a place where kids could meet and just be themselves. But in effect, it was after everything was over — the whole thing about youth getting together was probably dead by 1970. [The Centre] tried to do some programming. It tried to be a safe place. It tried to do in an organized sense what Middle Earth and a whole lot of other places across the country had been in a disorganized and spontaneous sense." (Crawley, March 19, 1990)

The Council's involvement as the support for staff and Management Committee of young people did, certainly, establish the Council as linked with the young and the radical as did their publication in 1968 of the Blue Book, a book of legal rights addressed primarily to transient youth. This book, an Alberta version of an original Yorkville Diggers publication, was sent to the Deputy Police Chief, Deputy Attorney General, the law faculty, and several other lawyers before publication. Nevertheless, when it was released it became a public controversy; the very fact that people were being told their rights was considered by some to be subversive. In addition, the language of the teens and the occasional editorializing on the law was found offensive:

There may be very good reasons to have changes made in the law concerning marijuana. We can point to academic studies showing the relative harmlessness of the drug. It is questionable that this justifies breaking the law. Clandestine use of marijuana is not civil disobedience, it's just a crime, besides a conviction on the charge of truancy is a quicker trip to martyrdom. (The Blue Book, 1968)

Besides giving the Council something of a reputation for supporting radicals, the work with youth also kept life exciting and a bit "offbeat" in the Council offices. When Rose French was hired as Office Manager — she was to be a mainstay of the office for over fifteen years — one of the departing secretaries informed her with some distaste that with all the strange people who used the office, she should take the precaution of washing her hands after using the telephone. Bettie Hewes recalls, with affectionate humour, trying to explain to Evelyn Battell, Director of the Teen Centre after Ed Delong had left, that there was no money for a project:

"Ev Battell wanted some more money for a youth program and I couldn't get any for her. She was furious with me. We shared the boardroom with the United Fund, great big table — shiny. I was at the end of my rope. I could do nothing more for her and she was very angry because there was always money for something, but there was never money for street kids. So she lay down on her back on the board table, like a beached whale, and started screaming the 'F' word at the top of her lungs.

I said, 'all right, all right, I'll get you anything. Stop.' I'd do anything." (Hewes, February 5, 1990)

As the youth centre project struggled ahead, the web of people being established around the Council was bringing in new materials concerning the latest theories of community and social action:

"We were part of a historical period . . . . There was a lot of information flow, a lot of cross-fertilization, a lot of networking going on. Part of it was Michel Blondin coming in with his stuff in terms of 'animation sociale', a different approach to community development than the Alinsky school. You had schools of community organizing that were peaking at that time . . . . There was Turner, *Freedom to Build*, that was one whole school of thought. Illich was just peaking, and Paulo Friere had written *Pedagogy of the Oppressed*. Theobald had several books and was just starting his 'dialogue-focusers' . . . . It was a time when a lot of community-based people-based theoretical things were just coming together in practice. Things people had been doing before now were legitimized. I think the Council really was a microcosm of that. The nice thing about it was, at that time, we had a lot of 'thinkers' on the Board and people who were pulling in new information." (Hannley, March 7, 1990)

One of those thinkers was Gerry Wright, Professor of Public Affairs in the Faculty of Extension at University of Alberta. His was one of the new voices heard on the Council's Board of Directors after the merger of the Youth Division and the Council, and for the

Council year 1968-69, he was President. He was intensely interested in the type of community change which was happening across North America, and in the thinking of those in the forefront, such as Robert Theobald. Wright brought Theobald to Edmonton, via the Faculty of Extension, to speak at the "Insight" Conference in 1969.

In this way, Theobald's views and his books, many of which dealt with the redistribution of wealth, became part of the "everyday" thinking of the Council's Board and staff. Two quotes, in particular, from Theobald's early books became almost emblematic of the thinking of many who worked for or with the Council at the time. The first was quoted on the cover of the Council's submission to the Worth Commission on Educational Planning:

> The possible is irrelevant, so it is only worth trying for the impossible. (Robert Theobald, *Education for a New Time*)

The second quote, from his book, *Toward An Alternative Future for America*, was first used in a series of internal reports on current projects to the Council Board in 1970. It was subsequently used in many external reports:

> I have developed an analogy about a train running on tracks headed over a cliff.

> Many of us are fighting to get at the controls. But the control board does not slow the train down. The only significant act, therefore, is to jump off the train, come together, get a helicopter and *leap far enough ahead of the train to lay a new set of tracks which leads away from the cliff.* (Robert Theobald)

In 1969, when Theobald visited Edmonton, society was coming to the end of a decade in which non-violence in the civil right's movement and anti-Vietnam movement was contrasted with violence in the almost regular assassinations of leaders and ghetto riots. Native leaders in Canada and separatists in Quebec were looking to the fortunes and techniques of the blacks in the United States as possible models for their own action. Neither Kent State nor the FLQ Crisis of October, 1970, had occurred, but for many, such events seemed possible. These two quotations from Theobald express the sense of profound crisis in society which pervaded much of the thinking at the Council, as well as the sense that major innovation was necessary for change, and the hope for a better future associated with the possibilities of human action.

These perceptions were expressed, not always in the choice of the particular projects on which the Council worked, but in the way in which it worked. Another of the early projects which came to the Council with Lynn Hannley, was in the familiar area of daycare with the "Growing Up Together Playschool" in the basement of Sacred Heart Church. It was felt that pre-school children in Boyle Street, particularly native children, needed some kind of enriched environment if they were to begin regular school on a level close to equal with their peers from other areas. The Growing Up Together mother's group was assisted to organize as a co-operative. While the mothers would not be required to volunteer in the playschool unless they wanted to, they were asked to direct the policy and planning of the play school, thus involving them as the primary decision-makers. This programme was unstructured and focused on developing a child's creativity through activities like painting, story-telling, and construction with play materials.

When Hannley approached All People's Mission with information about this project, Rev. George Spady sent an outraged letter to Stewart Bishop complaining that the Council was getting into the provision of direct services and explaining that the Mission was already planning a play school of its own. Stewart Bishop responded that while he understood Rev. Spady's concern, the Council's detached worker was free to organize as she saw fit.

For the Council, Growing Up Together, was not a direct service, although it was direct action. Rather it was an example of a familiar area of interest being approached in a different way. The steps here were first, listening to what the grassroots people had to say about their needs and the quality of services available, and second, using staff resources, sometimes quite intensively, to support the grassroots groups in trying out their own skills and achieving their own goals. Theoretical planning results were to be drawn from observing the action and results of the program. While the Growing Up Together Playschool lasted only a few months, it can be looked at as a model of one approach the Council was to use extensively for the next three to four years. In addition, it succeeded in identifying and supporting some of the community leadership, including women like Clara Big Charles who became active in subsequent projects as well as many of the members of the Native Brotherhood Society.

Identifying and supporting grassroots leadership was an important aspect of the Council's work, encouraged by the example of Michel

Blondin's "animation sociale". In 1968, the Council, with the sponsorship of the Canadian Welfare Council, brought Blondin from Montreal's Conseil des Oeuvres to talk about "animation sociale" with several groups in Edmonton. Quebec, was in the middle of its Quiet Revolution, and "animation sociale" had been developing since 1962-63 during a period of social ferment. The language used to describe its work was more radical than that being developed by the fledgling community development movement in Edmonton, and it had already had time to analyze some of its methods, successes, and failures.

Blondin's paper *"Animation Sociale" as Developed and Practised by Le Conseil Des Oeuvres De Montreal*, October 1968, became an important text for the work in Edmonton. It described in considerable detail the central objective of social animation — participation — operational objectives, the methodology, role of the "animateur", and the Citizens' Committee, as well as analyzing the work to date in Montreal. In summarizing the lessons learned already through the social animation work, Blondin said,

> But the most important results, in our view, stem from the creation of local leadership, which is trying to gradually spread its influence through the district and transform it. These new leaders have begun to gain self-confidence and discover their strength, to experience the birth of a hope which gives them the strength to undertake great tasks. These same leaders are gradually developing their social consciousness and are becoming capable of understanding and interpreting many events whose ramifications extend far beyond their own district.

This concentration on participation and the development of leadership among the groups of disadvantaged people in a community became an important theme of the Council's work over the next decade. One of the groups where this was particularly true was in the single unemployed male/transient/urban native community in Boyle Street. The work of Lynn Hannley and Father Marc brought the Council very direct contact with this community. Together they supported and assisted the formation of the Native Brotherhood Society, led by George McDermott.

The Brotherhood took over the running of the Boyle Street Information Centre started by the urban renewal department. This storefront drop-in and information centre provided coffee, warmth, and companionship, as well as information to anyone who walked in. It also provided a location in which people from all walks of life compared notes and began the conversations which led to new action. For example, the first seeds of what would later become the Boyle Street Community Services Co-operative were planted in a conversation between a concerned public health nurse, Margaret Bouska, who had come to the Centre to find out what it could do for her patients, and Lynn Hannley, early in the winter of 1970.

Meanwhile, the United Community Fund had requested that the Council bring the various agencies in Boyle Street together and do a study of needs and services. The Council agreed, but included a new constituency in this study. Father Marc had been working closely with several groups of non-native transient men and was assisting them to organize into self-help organizations such as the City Centre Co-operative Club and the Community Upgrading and Rehabilitation Edmonton Society (CURES):

> Father Marc gave a comprehensive picture of work with transient men and he described the process of redeveloping the City Centre Cooperative Club, the membership of which is comprised of men living on skid row. This group has a discussion every Monday. One of its main objectives is finding employment. Father Marc noted that most of the men have many personal problems. He described some of the difficulties in employment . . . . He also stated that one of the biggest problems is to stabilize these men. Because of their mobile transitory method of living it was very difficult to build social relationships. (Minutes, Board of Directors, November 24, 1969).

Members of these groups, along with others who frequented the Boyle Street Information Centre, and almost all of whom stayed at one of the hostels in the area, became the grassroots constituency consulted by the Council about needs and services. They were encouraged to write briefs and to go to speak with the politicians themselves, although often with a Community Worker close at hand. In spring 1968, CURES, for example, sent a brief to the government making recommendations for a rehabilitation programme for transients, beginning with a classification centre at the hostels and including community house accommodations for those in the programme. That Brief began,

> *Transients* are described as men without jobs, money or homes — men on skid-row for a complexity of reasons. All have one

common motivation on entering skid-row — to seek shelter and food. Hence, their coming to hostels.

Once in the hostels, the men are trapped . . . thrown into a pack without a thorough understanding of the exact nature of their problems or of their needs to get out of skid-row. It is left to the strong to overcome a great number of difficulties and to the weak to resign themselves either to a fate no less than pitiful co-existence in a fruitless transient society or to suicide. (*A Dream of Things that Never Were*, Sept. 1968)

A few months later, the CURES Brief became the basis for a Council proposal, *A Dream of Things that Never Were*, to the Human Resources Development Authority. Again, the request was for funding for a Classification Centre and for separate housing for the younger men. Funding was not forthcoming; however, largely because of the activity of these men, the issue of services for transients was kept a public issue for some time. Incidents of violence, especially at the hostel, were complained of so frequently and publicly that the province set up a Judicial Inquiry into the Single Men's Hostel. The Council made a statement to Mr. Justice O'Byrne's Inquiry setting out the Council's position that a complete overhaul of services and service philosophy was necessary:

There is little evidence that the services provided individually or collectively have made any change in the living conditions or life styles of the men concerned; *if change and rehabilitation are the objectives — the system is not working.*

As a result, we are now studying the situation from the position of the men who are in it and members of the Planning Council are linking up with the men individually and in groups to explore solutions together. Our study is not static, not psychological or sociological, study and process become one and the same . . . .

It is our belief that the system including both public and private services, not only maintains and increases the dependency of the men but also reinforces their transiency and isolation.

In our current analysis we are convinced that a re-design of services is required. We are further convinced that the effectiveness of the system is dependent upon the continuous involvement of the men themselves in both planning and management. (Statement

of the Edmonton Social Planning Council to the Honourable Mr.
Justice O'Byrne, Re: Single Men's Hostel)

It was in developing this material, and a subsequent brief to the Senate
Committee on Poverty, that Father Marc coined the phrase, "the skid-
row concentration camp" to describe his contention that the prolifera-
tion of small single purpose services in Boyle Street literally forced
the unemployed male to be transient each and every day, to travel
through a circle of services which would provide enough to allow him
to move to the next service, but not enough to move outside of the
circle. This model became central to the Council's thinking about skid
row and supported the Council's call for a total restructuring of
services.

Justice O'Byrne's report did recommend changes, but not the sweeping changes the Council had suggested. The provincial government
responded with a proposal to privatize the hostel through a Request-
For-Proposal system. The men of the City Centre Co-operative Club
opposed privatization as did the Council, chiefly on the grounds that
social services could not be run as businesses with a goal of maximiz-
ing profit without seriously undermining services. The organized
opposition in Edmonton was sufficient that the Edmonton hostel was
not privatized.

The Council worked on several other projects related to the problems of the men on skid row as well, always attempting to experiment with new ways of providing services. On March 16, 1970, there
were four projects suggested to the Board, three of which were based
in Boyle Street:

a) An employment service to be operated by Mr. Bill Grover [a skid
   row man himself] on a three month trial basis at $50 per week.
c) The FUTURE Society — a self help group of convicts and
   ex-convicts — financial support is required to help pay for one
   worker. The Council's proposed share to be $100 per month
   for six months.
d) Community Newspaper — Mr. Bruce Sloan [a retiree, resident in the Boyle Street Area] requested the Council's sponsorship of a newsletter/newspaper to give information, carry
   ads re jobs, and emphasize in its content the need to bridge
   the gap between recipients of welfare and welfare services and
   those who are in charge with [sic] administering.(Board
   Minutes, March 16, 1970)

These projects were accepted by the Board, and money not spent in other areas were used to support them. In each case, the Council was experimenting with the use of workers who were indigenous to the community and the culture of those they were trying to assist. These projects tended to be successful in achieving their particular objects at first, but to depend largely on the enthusiasm and personality of the original indigenous worker for their success.

The Women's Overnight Emergency Shelter Project, on the other hand, depended on group leadership from the beginning, and has continued and adapted until the present. In 1968, a committee of interested citizens, primarily from church groups and chaired by Ron Mossman, had researched the situation of homeless women in Edmonton and presented its findings in the Mossman Report. Critical among the findings were the facts that there were regularly many more homeless women than there were emergency beds, and that the existing services would only accept women who were sober. The response to this report was to set up a management committee that would implement the Mossman recommendations, specifically

> . . . that we provide a drop-in information and placement service from 4:30 to 9:00 p.m. combined with emergency sit-up shelter services from 9:00 p.m. to 9:00 a.m., seven days a week on a three month trial basis. (Shelter Proposal, 1969)

The resulting shelter, run first under the umbrella of the YWCA and later the Council, was staffed by volunteers, along with one paid staff, during the hours of 4:30 p.m. to 9:00 a.m. During the three-month trial 80 volunteers worked at the Shelter for 1,966 hours. The Social Planning Council provided intensive staff assistance for the shelter, particularly for the training of the large volunteer corps. Middle class women, from church groups and service clubs, needed to learn to be at ease with and responsive to some of the toughest women from skid row, since the Shelter was the refuge of last resort.

The most effective training tool was the Women's Shelter game, developed by Council staff, to simulate life for a woman on skid row. Following the skid row concentration camp model, the Shelter game was a kind of circular "Snakes and Ladders" in which the object was to escape the circle, but each step in the circle made escape more difficult. At an average training session, the volunteers would begin expressing their personal frustration with the "no-win" situation after about five minutes of play, and by 10 minutes, had generalized this frustration into an understanding of, and often identification with, the rage of the skid row women. In consequence, apart from its service to homeless women, the Shelter project also developed a large group of middle class women who felt a shared experience with the homeless and who were equally comfortable being part of a meeting with a Cabinet Minister in his office or a protest march on the steps of the Legislature. Many of these women continued on to become significant members of the Council Board and other Council projects as well, thus giving the Council a depth of community support that was important for its own survival.

At the same time, the Shelter project caused considerable tension between the United Community Fund and the Council. Even before the Shelter became an issue, tensions between the two organizations had risen when the Council Board under Gerry Wright and Joe Donahue had requested Stewart Bishop's resignation. The Fund, in its turn, hired Bishop to staff a new planning section of its own and tried to reduce the Planning Council's financial allotment by the amount of Bishop's salary.

The Shelter became one of the issues where these tensions were played out. Because the Shelter accepted any woman under any circumstances, its clientele often included women who had been thrown out of rehabilitative services for women. Thus, by its very existence, the Shelter became a kind of de facto critique of the other agencies:

"We started the first one [shelter] in the Anglican church . . . but the YWCA became anxious, the Fund became anxious. The perception was that all we had to do for any woman who was homeless was find her a home and she would immediately become a woman established. We know, of course, that that isn't the way humanity works.

Anyway, because we were supporting the notion of a shelter, the United Fund threatened us, and said 'we are going to do a study'. So they did a Study and it revealed that there were all these services for women and they were on a sort of ladder, and women could climb up this ladder and presumably marry a doctor at the top! Something along those lines. [The Study concluded that] these were enough services and that a shelter wasn't needed. It perpetuated something rather than intervened. They revealed this Study, with the implication that we were going to be cut off.

We dug in, and fortunately, we had enough of the Ardis' and the Margs and the Jessicas who had the credibility in their community to make the United Fund take a second look. So the Shelter continued to operate. There was immense anxiety over it. But churches all across the community supported it, and gradually Art Holmes took it over and parlayed it into the shelter that the province runs. And that [original] group went on and founded WIN House." (Hewes, February 5, 1990).

Several other major projects illustrate the Council's work from 1968 to 1972, under Hewes' direction: the development of the Retired and Semi-retired Society, the Humans on Welfare Society (HOW), the Disabled Action Group, the Boyle Street Community Services Co-operative, and the Housing Charette which began co-operative housing in Edmonton. In each of these cases, there was a determination to work directly with the people who were concerned with the issue, and to develop new, more effective ways of working on such issues.

The organization of HOW, the Retired and Semi-retired Society, and the Disabled Action Group were again projects in which the Council was working with traditional issues but dealing directly with the people concerned. Hewes describes the first meeting of what would become the Disabled Action Group, as the new ways of working met the old, literally in the same room:

"We'd decided that disabled people didn't have any control over their lives at all. Edna Laforge was head of the Multiple Sclerosis Society. She was to be the chair of a meeting called of folks who wanted to talk about taking some control of where they lived.

The meeting was in the Mercantile Building which was inaccessible [to wheelchairs]. It had an elevator, but stairs down into the board room, stairs everywhere. We must have had 30 or 40 wheelchairs. The meeting was delayed more than 3/4 of an hour because they couldn't get more than two wheelchairs in the elevator at a time. They just jammed the place.

Edna knew them all, but she knew them as docile people in wheelchairs. She didn't know them as aggressive, mobilized, change agents. The meeting was just barely under control. There was an undercurrent of 'we can do it, we will, and nobody will stand in our way'. Quite a remarkable change." (Hewes, February 5, 1990)

This group grew from that first meeting to a dynamic action group which had many accomplishments, including initiating the development of its own independent housing project.

The Boyle Street Community Services Co-operative grew out of the work of the Native Brotherhood Society-Boyle Street Information Centre, and the large group of professionals, community workers, and Boyle Street residents who congregated around the Information Centre. This was a time when there was "a pre-occupation with co-ordination, restructuring, and re-organizing what was seen as a haphazard arrangement of services". (Keith Wass, Speech to ESPC Annual Meeting, May 21, 1980) Certainly, the growth of services in Boyle Street had appeared haphazard and the residents still found services to be inaccessible. The Council, with the Native Brotherhood, brought together meetings of all the appropriate agencies, planned the project, and applied for funding for a three-year pilot project from the Department of Health and Welfare. While the planning was going on, John Munro, the federal Minister of Health and Welfare came to Edmonton; the Council attempted to schedule a meeting with him, but the only available time was early in the morning while driving the Minister to the airport:

"Dave King arranged the meeting. I was the 'introducer'. David was driving and trying to talk at the same time — all on icy roads. Lynn made one presentation; Roger Poppe made one, and Alice [Bartels] made one. That's how the Boyle Street Co-op got funded . . . . Munro was impressed. His comment when he got to the airport was 'I've never had a presentation that was so clear and so well-defined. Come on into the VIP lounge and I'll introduce you to my Executive Assistant.'" (Interview, Joe Donahue, February 20, 1990)

The original intention of this project was to bring all the major services for the area under one roof and under the direction of a co-operative society made up of residents. While this intention was never wholly fulfilled, in that the various public and private services were not prepared to subordinate their workers to a community Board, nevertheless it has provided a centralized core of information, counselling, and advocacy in the neighbourhood for eighteen years.

In a very real sense, the Housing Charette grew out of the Boyle Street Information project as well. In the first days of community development work, Lynn Hannley and others had realized that housing was one of the major problems of the area:

"It all started through the Native Brotherhood. We were doing things for the Hellyer Task Force [on Housing] and then people said 'why don't we solve our own housing problem. We're tired of doing briefs and reports for government.' So we started looking for models.

At the same time, a group of people came together — at the first meeting we had about 25 people because housing was such a significant issue. Lillian Piche was getting kicked out of her house because rents were going up. So we looked and looked and couldn't find her a place. She was native, a single mom. What we had to do was make a public statement.

So we got a teepee and set it up in Churchill Square. That teepee was there for about two weeks, and they lived there. It was part of the times to make big public statements and the Council and Gerry Wright were all involved. This caused a lot of consternation. 'How dare we do such a thing!' So that was how housing became a public issue." (Hannley, March 7, 1990)

Out of the teepee demonstration, a group of people, including several of the women from the Growing Up Together playschool, formed the Edmonton Citizens' for Better Housing (ECBH), an organization dedicated to working on housing issues on a broad scale. Under the umbrella of ECBH, the first housing registry for Edmonton was operated, a Housing Month was proclaimed, and briefs to governments were written on several issues.

The core interest of this group became the development of housing co-operatives as a way of developing housing for people with low incomes. The group set to work researching all types of housing co-operatives and also models for planning such housing communities. It decided to hold a 'charette' in June 1970.

The 'charette' was an intensive planning process, based originally on the habit the Parisian architectural college students had of completing their projects while being driven to the college in a "charette", a horse-drawn buggy. As used in the United States for community school and hospital planning, it was a time-limited planning process (usually one or two weeks) in which the service users came together daily with all of the experts involved, and plans were to be developed from overall goals to the end product.

The Sturgeon Valley Housing Charette was a 10 day process, during which approximately 50 potential residents met at 5 p.m. each day with city planners, architects, education, recreation, and transportation experts; shared supper together; then carried out the particular planning tasks set for that day. Several Council staff including Lynn Hannley, Marsha Mitchell, and Bettie Hewes, as well as seven full-time Council volunteers worked on the planning of this charette in the orange-carpeted, cork-walled "playroom" which Gerry Wright had built in the back of the Council office. The Council lent ECBH $5,000 to carry out the project, and the group, in turn, received a grant from Central Mortgage and Housing. The charette proved to be a very valuable technique for planning, and was subsequently used with the Disabled Action Group in developing their housing plan and in the Whyte Avenue area to work on community planning.

There were several other projects which began during this period, including one of the first of the 1970s women's conferences across the country, 'I, A Woman Today'. There was also an active group, led by Marsha Mitchell, involved in developing a community-based rehabilitation programme and alternative to prison for women. The federal employment programmes, Opportunities for Youth (OFY) and Local Initiatives Programmes (LIP), provided a relatively accessible kind of no-strings funding which enabled many groups to pursue, for brief periods, their immediate goals. In addition, however, the Council's philosophy supported the development of such group projects:

"What was interesting about the Council was that as these issues surfaced — and they were legitimate issues because all of a sudden it was legitimate for interest groups to express themselves — it was able to respond to a variety of different needs. It was open and it had developed the 'raison d'etre' to be the facilitator to help people move from A to B. So whoever came in the door, as long as they had a legitimate issue, was worked with." (Hannley, March 7, 1990)

Not everyone, however, was content with this approach. Many of the more traditional social agencies, including the United Community Fund, felt the sting of the citizens' group critiques and harboured a sense that the Council had somehow betrayed them. In addition, within the Council's extended web of associates there was a growing feeling that there was not enough focus in this approach. Such a feeling was expressed by Peter Boothroyd, who was to become the next Executive Director of the Council:

"There was a lot of anxiety among the Board members . . .that there wasn't a clear enough direction for the Council at this point. What they had been doing under Bettie's [Hewes] guidance had been, largely, I think, responding to a great number of opportunities which at that time were just opening up as a result of all the make-work programs. So very energetically, Bettie and some other people had been helping a lot of groups get started. Some very good ones . . . But there was some question — how do you decide who to help and who not to help? (Interview, Peter Boothroyd, April 8, 1990) Concurrently with this philosophical questioning, the Council staff of the 68-72 period resigned between the fall of '71 and fall of '72. Thus, by the end of 1972 the Council had a complete change of staff, a rewritten Constitution, and a very much refocused direction."

Changing Voices — Summary

The decade of the sixties was a decade of change for every institution in North America, and the Council was no exception. The first change, and one of the most important, was the structural separation from the Community Chest which came with the creation of a United Community Fund. With this separation, the Council became freer to pursue those issues which it saw as most crucial without immediate reference to the views of the funding agency, which because of its dependence on corporate donations, tended to view society in business terms. At the same time, this change also left the Council itself more vulnerable to cuts in its own funding. This is not to say that the Council became unrealistically radical. During the first eight years of the sixties, the major constituencies of the Council — seniors and the disabled; youth, pre-schoolers, and UCF agencies — were the traditional constituencies.

While this work was taking place, however, the motivating ideas behind Council work were changing. New Board members, several drawn from the Youth Division when it merged with the Senior Council, were excited by and involved with the leading edge of social thinking from across the continent. Consequently, the methods of working, both within the Council staff and Board as well as with its various constituencies, changed. Starting in the early sixties, the philosophies of community development — that is, listening primarily to the voices of the poor and disadvantaged for their information about needs and solutions and developing leadership from within those communities — gradually became the central philosophies of the Council. Thus, by 1968, the Council hired its own community development worker, and began to work, particularly within the Boyle Street area, directly with the native, the transient, the female, and youth communities. The voices of the Council, as they spoke to the public, to government, and to the voluntary sector, became more and more identified with the voices of the disadvantaged. From the mid-sixties onward as well, the Council began to work very specifically with physical planning issues, such as urban renewal, parks planning, and housing — especially co-operative housing, believing that such physical issues were critical to human welfare.

The focus on urban issues was to become the central focus of the 1970s.

Section Four

1972 – 79:
Strategies for Survival

Chapter Fourteen

Urban Gladiators

Although the actions of the Council in the late 1960s had already demonstrated its image as an agent of change, the Council members who came to the Annual Meeting in May 1972 were prepared to formalize that image. The new Objects of the Council were much simplified in form:

The Edmonton Social Planning Council is an agent for social change and development.

An objective of the organization is to develop and maintain a voluntary non-governmental capability for informed decision-making and action.

The Council provides resources to initiate and also to support efforts through which citizen plans can be developed and implemented. (ESPC By-laws)

An equally critical change was that the egalitarian approach to work, which had earlier been adopted by the staff and most Board members, was formally extended to the structure of the Council at the May 1972 Annual General Meeting. The traditional Board of Directors and President structure was replaced by a co-ordinating group of 10 elected members led by a group of three Co-chairs, who would rotate the presidential tasks among them. This careful rotation of tasks went as far as picking a Chair of the Day and Recorder of the Day for each Co-ordinating Group meeting. The other egalitarian change in the by-laws permitted Council staff to be full voting members of the Co-ordinating Group.

As the constitution was changed, so also the dominant personalities in the Council were changing. Roger Soderstrom, although a longtime member of the Council, was taking a more active role in Council work in the late sixties and early seventies. In 1971, he followed Joe Donahue as President of the Council. At the time, as well as being heavily involved with the Council, Soderstrom was enrolled in graduate studies in community development at the University of Alberta, and subsequently wrote *Edmonton Social Planning Council: An Analysis 1928 - 1975* as his M.A. thesis. Understandably, his orientation to Council work was a somewhat more academic one than that of his predecessors. Then in 1972, after a brief stint as one of the Co-chairs of the Co-ordinating Group, he joined the staff of the Council as one of the planners.

Also in 1972, Peter Boothroyd replaced Bettie Hewes as the senior staff of the Council, taking the title of Co-ordinator rather than Executive Director, in keeping with the egalitarian direction of the constitutional change.

> Mr. Boothroyd came to the Council with a very different background. He was not a social worker and could most accurately be called an urban sociologist. Because of this urban orientation, the Council took on a wider focus than the traditional areas of Council concern in health, social services and recreation. Urban planning, urban environment and participatory democracy became additional issues to focus on. (Soderstrom, Edmonton Social Planning Council: An Analysis, 1976)

Prior to joining the Council staff, Boothroyd had been part of a think tank, developing policy initiatives for the provincial Social Credit government. He was also a part of Gerry Wright's Extension Department practicum in urban transportation, which was developing the fundamental research documents on freeways and light rapid transit in the city.

> "I knew Peter at University in Graduate Studies, and I also knew Peter by reason of [his] being part of that SocCred advisory group. Then he surprised me by taking this job [with the ESPC]. I was delighted. He and I were really good buddies at the time, colleagues in the revolution. I thought 'what a capture, to get a mind like this at the Council'. And it was. He gave oodles of his time and energy and intelligence, and that meant a lot of good leadership." (Wright, February 8, 1990)

The third relatively new face to Council leadership was Leslie Bella, who was a community development worker for the City of Edmonton Social Services:

> "I was involved with one of the high schools, M. E. Lazerte, when

it was just opening, and there was a move to make it a more community-based high school . . . . As a community worker with the city, I became involved in that process. There was a group based in the Social Planning Council who were also interested in and concerned about community education and the community school concept." (Interview, Leslie Bella, April 12, 1990)

Bella had come to Edmonton from Vancouver, where she had been involved with The Electors' Action Movement (TEAM), an urban political party formed primarily in reaction to proposals for freeway development. She had been elected as a board member at the same time as Roger Soderstrom was elected President, and after the next Annual Meeting, became another of the Co-chairs of the Council.

Thus in 1972, the first full year of operation under the new Constitution, there was a new wave of leadership. Boothroyd and Soderstrom were on staff, and a third planner, Deloris Russell, who had previously worked with Council and Women's Shelter projects, was hired. The Co-ordinating Group was led by the Co-chairs: Gerry Wright, Leslie Bella, and Ron Mossman who was also the Chair of the Women's Emergency Shelter Society. This new leadership brought with them a strong orientation toward urban issues and toward a research approach to social action and social change:

> The Council then became more task than process-oriented . . . . its basic change strategy stressed fact-gathering and report writing. The new staff saw the previous process orientation of the Council as a never-ending mire of involvement with ever-continuing projects where objectives were neither stated nor articulated. The task forces [an approach to report development] were really an attempt to define problems and issues more clearly, which is a social planning approach. But at the same time citizen involvement in the resolution of the problem . . . was encouraged. It was hoped that by pulling together individuals in the community in task forces and feeding them relevant data, social change could be achieved by the Council's assuming an advocacy role. Thus through task force reports and their release, the Council would affect the decisions of government, 'funds', and private agencies. (Soderstrom, Edmonton Social Planning Council: An Analysis, 1976)

In order to focus on what it saw as a more effective task-oriented approach, the Council developed, during 1972, a diagram which presented the main areas of social concern which they saw as primary for the Council, the types of activity possible, and the degree of social change orientation which they could expect. Within this diagram, future Council work could be located and assessed according to its appropriateness and effectiveness.

Four Citizens' Commissions were formed within the Council 'whose responsibility it [was] to continuously explore present social policies, to recommend social objectives and to appraise the community's progress in reaching these objectives' (Annual Report, 1972). Each of these Commissions was to work in one of the major areas of social concern:

Participatory Democracy, which includes concern with the accessibility of public information, the success of community councils and the development of mechanisms to link citizens and officials.

Decent Standard of Living, which includes concern about the present patchwork of welfare programs and their collective inadequacy to eliminate poverty, the continuing difficulty for many in getting complete and proper health care and the very low wages for which too many people work.

Humane Social Controls, including concerns about our present treatment of criminal offenders, alcoholics, drug addicts, transients, the mentally ill and children.

Humane Urban Environment, focusing on the social consequences of our choices for urban transportation, neighbourhood and downtown design, and the questionable adequacy of present housing standards and supply. (Annual Report, 1972)

Within these Commissions, which, it was planned, would report once a year, Task Forces of people interested in particular issues were set up, to do research and write Task Force reports as the basis for citizen action. In addition, staff would conduct various research studies, and where possible, additional staff would be hired under particular project grants.

Even before the structure and new leadership was complete, however, one other element of the work of this period in the Council became obvious and somewhat troublesome; that was the approach of active politics as Leslie Bella remembers it:

"There were two threads [of motivating ideas] which I could particularly pick up. One was a citizen participation, community involvement, citizen action, a kind of progressive-liberal-democratic approach which was definitely underlying a lot of what was said and a lot that was done during that period. It actually reflected itself in the things that URGE ultimately promoted in terms of the ward system. It was also part of the Mayor's Conference on Citizen Participation which also had some shared personnel with the Planning Council. That was definitely one element.

But there was also a more critical thread, more of an undercurrent and less overt I think, of a desire to change things, that was more concerned with getting the change than the democratic nature of that change. Sometimes we'd have a citizen involvement project that we'd all get excited about, but my sense was, that there were other people who thought, 'we've got to change some of these things and all the involvement in the world isn't going to produce the change.'

It's from that, for many of us, that the limits of the Social Planning Council became quite obvious. We could involve people, we could talk a lot, we could present good ideas, we could promote progressive planning and all that type of thing, but all we could do from the Council was talk and promote, not actually change. So a number of us drifted toward politics." (Bella, April 12, 1990)

As early as the mid-sixties, the Council had been looking at the issue of community schools as well as the community use of school premises. As the municipal elections of autumn 1971 drew closer, the Council decided to host a public forum for School Board candidates to discuss their positions on community schools. The material which was sent out to advertise the forum indicated which candidates supported community schools and implicitly, if not explicitly, indicated Council support. The United Community Fund was incensed:

In light of the pamphlet which you enclosed with your letter and which had been read by several Board members, together with press statements, . . . members of the Board are of the firm opinion that the Social Planning Council was directly involved in a political campaign. I might also add that a number of individuals, as well as some UCF agencies, voiced serious objections to the Social Planning Council's involvement in these elections. (letter, John Schlosser, President, United Community Fund to Roger Soderstrom, President, ESPC, October 28, 1971.

Certainly, some members of the Council were intending solid support for certain school board candidates:

"The Separate School Board set up a project [community school] based in the inner city school. That's where the Social Planning Council became involved in School Board elections to attempt to raise the possibility of community schools through the electoral process. I suppose we were all pretty naive, but we got into serious trouble with the United Community Fund, who said we shouldn't be messing around with politics . . . . Part of the problem was that one of our candidates, Leo Floyd, won. So it was a big issue.

Subsequently when we set up the Urban Reform Group — we were less naive by the time we set up URGE — we kept the Social Planning Council clean even though that was the point of contact for many of the people." (Bella, April 12, 1990)

There was some difficulty, after the election, in even arranging a meeting with the Board of the United Fund in order to discuss their complaints; however, after considerable effort on the part of the Council, the matter seemed to be laid to rest. Leslie Bella was appointed as a Council representative on the Fund's Board and relations between the Council and Fund were temporarily eased.

Despite giving up the overt political approach to education issues, the Council continued with studies of the current state of community schools, Task Force reports on school drop-outs, day care, and on the province's "Operational Plans for Early Childhood Services". In addition, the Council wrote and published a handbook, *The Sunclimbers*, on developing parent-run co-operative pre-school programs. The introduction to *The Sunclimbers* demonstrates the Council's philosophy of promoting community action and control:

If you take part in creating a pre-school for your child, the picture is an entirely different one [from a private kindergarten or publicly sponsored pre-school]. Not only will you know very well what he does there and why, you will also be responsible in part for deciding the activities and approach to be used and for choosing the kind of person who will be his teacher. (*The Sunclimbers*, 1972).

Also in 1972, one major research project in the key area of 'Decent Standard of Living' was being carried out by Ted Parnell, hired especially for this study. It was an effort by the Council "to be in a position to lead policy development not simply react to government proposals relative to this subject" (Co-ordinating Committee Minutes, Sept. 7, 1972). It is important to note that this report was the first major Council document on poverty and social assistance published after the election of the Progressive Conservative government. The change in provincial government in the autumn of 1971 presented the Council with a major change in both the personalities and the approach of the government:

"After Peter Lougheed was elected Premier, and saw the difference between services in other provinces and in Alberta — I'm told he made up his mind he was going to have the best civil service in the country. He had the oil money to pay for it, and it burgeoned into a wide range of services. Because of that, new people came into the field who didn't know the Social Planning Council, and were not necessarily familiar with the traditions of how things had evolved and they began inventing their own [rules]. So the central position in which the Council had found itself had eroded." (Bishop, March 7, 1990)

To attempt to engage in any serious dialogue with this newly sophisticated Department of Social Development would require more sophisticated presentations. With the publication of *Alternatives to Poverty and Welfare in Alberta*, the Council achieved the goal of a sophisticated piece of research which did present clear policy alternatives. It looked carefully at the statistics of poverty, the effects of social and economic policies on the poor, the income security programs available and the welfare system in Alberta, before recommending a Guaranteed Annual Income with work incentives. This document formed a solid basis for much of the Council's work on poverty for the next several years.

As the seventies progressed, particularly after the oil crisis of 1973, Alberta lived in a world of economic boom and high inflation. The Citizens' Commission on Decent Standard of Living was operating in an economic environment where those who were employed were likely to have relatively high incomes, while those on fixed incomes or public assistance were becoming poorer. Thus, a good deal of this Commission's work, based on the *Alternatives to Poverty and Welfare in Alberta*, focused on promoting the Guaranteed Annual Income as a way of redistributing the wealth.

Among the Task Forces which reported within this area was the Task Force on *The Public Assistance Food Allowance Increase*. Typical of the Task Force approach, this Task Force was formed to respond briefly and quickly to a specific issue, in this case the Department of Social Development's 9 per cent increase in food allowance as of May 1, 1973. The Task Force report began with a statistical analysis of the increase, pointing out its inadequacy when measured against a 14.6 per cent increase in the price of food in the preceding 16 months. The four-page report ended by identifying seven problem areas for the Department of Health and Social Development to study in order to alleviate problems of poor nutrition and increasing poverty. Also based on the Decent Standard of Living research, the Council published two books for use in schools: *Twenty Questions on Welfare* and *To Be Poor in Canada*.

The Citizens' Commission on Humane Social Controls worked for two years developing its major report covering the entire system of justice from police, individual liberties, bail, and legal aid to sentencing, after-care and special groups of offenders. Throughout the report, *Justice in Alberta: A Citizen's Look at the Law*, the writers described in detail the system as it existed and provided many alternatives, most of these relating to ways of increasing the involvement of the community in developing effective approaches to social control.

Briefs on citizen participation and community councils, along with a Community Council Handbook were major products of the Citizens' Commission on Participatory Democracy. Beginning in 1968 with the formation of the Mayor's Committee on Human Resources, the idea of community councils, which would supervise co-ordinated social, health, recreation, and other human services for a particular area, was explored in Edmonton. In 1971, a community service centre, West 10, with just such a community council was set up as a pilot project. The Council had maintained a representative on the Mayor's Committee and supported West 10 throughout its existence. However, the Council wanted to see community councils formed in all areas of the city with much broader powers and responsibilities than the community council associated with West 10:

The actual design of a community council structure proposed in this submission is predicated on the following assumptions:
1. the community council structure should to the fullest extent possible make use of existing structures,
2. the community councils should be concerned with the complete development of their communities in terms of physical and social aspects,
3. different kinds of concern or activities are best dealt with, or organized by, different sized communities.(Submission re Community Councils, March 1975)

The Council proposed that the existing community league structure would be the base for the development of such community councils, and that a new Community Development Agency be set up to provide community development workers for the community councils. City Council, however, was not entirely happy with the operation of West 10 and did not renew the project after the three year trial:

The Area Council had a very difficult time for the three years, and eventually saw themselves as an advisory committee with no real authority over the 50 or so staff assigned in from other jurisdictions. The Provincial Department retained strict supervisory control over their staff, and to a lesser degree, the same happened with other staff.

Another development that started out as positive, turned out just the opposite. The project was highly successful in obtaining a lot of extra staff from temporary funding projects . . . , and this added an extra level of service far beyond what was provided in other areas of the City. Some Aldermen began to question what we were moving toward. [Was] another political level to be established under area councils in various areas of the City? Thus despite some degree of success, the project was abandoned. (Wass, Address to Annual Meeting, 1980)

With the end of the West 10 project, the hopes for the establishment of other community councils disappeared. One of the lasting contributions of the work of West 10 along with the Council, however, was the preparation of *Rape of the Block* (or everyperson's guide to neighbourhood defense) with funding from an LIP grant:

Written by Missy Parnell, Verna Semotuk and Joan Swain after six months of investigation and behind-the-scenes prying, it takes a light-hearted look at areas of everyday relevance to everyday citizens. It is well-sprinkled with cartoons and illustrations by local artist, Harry Savage . . . .

Included is a citizen's guide to avoiding City Hall red tape, a few pointers on putting pressure on the powers that be, a brief run-down of active community groups, an article on the advantages of establishing community councils, and the ins and outs of pro-tecting your neighbourhood. (Annual Report, 1974)

Rape of the Block became a kind of citizens' best seller, used by many community groups in Edmonton over the next few years, and sold to activist citizens as far away as Toronto.

It was, however, through the work under the Commission on Humane Urban Environment that the Council had its greatest impact during this period. The Commission itself, with staff help from Batya Chivers who was hired for specific projects in this area, worked on developing a citizens' general plan for the city. Other projects included considerable research into proposals for the river valley, including *An Approach to Planning River Valley Trails*, funded by the Alberta Environ-mental Research Trust (AERT), and a study proposing the develop-ment of mini-parks, also funded by the AERT, and written by Leslie Bella. Others in the Council, particularly Peter Boothroyd and Gerry Wright, concentrated on the problems of urban transportation.

From his earliest days with the Council, Gerry Wright had been interested in the physical aspects of planning as they affected the social fabric of the city. Through the Faculty of Extension, he organized several Research Practicums "as a community leadership development program" (Lightbody and Wright, Urban Innovation? Conditions Underpinning the Transformation of Movement into Party: The Case of the Urban Reform Group of Edmonton, prepared for FAUI Workshop, Paris, 1989)

While the Research Practicum played the role of the main researcher for the citizens' groups, the Council played the role of strategic co-ordination of the varied community groups and their efforts. By the time of the second set of public hearings on the transportation plans, in November 1972, "57 citizens groups appeared, and 54 spoke with one voice since all were linked informationally to either the University Practicums or the Edmonton Social Planning Council, or both". (Lightbody and Wright, 1989). From 1972 through 1974, the Council operated in two main areas: a) making its own submissions on particular transportation alternatives; b) carrying out public education for citizens in the transportation arena and consulting with City of Edmonton planners in respect to obtaining citizen participation in the creation of transportation plans. Along with other community groups, the Council hosted a Citizens' Transportation Planning Conference in 1974 at which 130 participants developed resolutions:

> The steering committee of the conference, through Peter Boothroyd, spoke to the hearing on the transportation bylaw and succeeded in securing certain guarantees in this bylaw that the City's policy favouring public transit and indicating safeguards for neighbourhoods and ravines would be respected by the City. (Annual Report, 1974)

The city's transportation plan, with its Light Rail Transit system and its modest freeway network reflects much of the work of the various citizens' groups of that time, particularly the Council and the Faculty of Extension practicums, although it also reflects important changes in municipal politics heralded by the formation of URGE:

> In the summer of 1973 the 'urban gladiators' operating at the centre of the information network in the ESPC and the University decided that in spite of some specific successes their alternative vision of the 'good city' would prevail only if the citizen groups could run candidates and gain seats on city council. (Lightbody and Wright, 1989)

Several of the people involved, in particular Gerry Wright, Peter Boothroyd, and Leslie Bella, went on to be founding members of URGE. Thus, as the key leadership of the 1972-1974 period at the Council moved on to become part of an active political movement, the way was left open for another approach to social planning for the 1970s.

Chapter Fifteen

Under Siege

While the Fund's disapproval of some of the Council's projects in the late 60s and early 70s had been temporarily assuaged, and the outright conflict between the United Community Fund and the Council over the School Board elections had subsided, relations between the two organizations were still not smooth. The more successful — and publicly successful — the Planning Council became in its urban design and transportation campaigns and in its support of the burgeoning neighbourhood groups, the more uneasy the United Way (name changed in 1973) became. In addition, there was an undercurrent of power struggle as the United Way's new planning section carved out for itself the agency co-ordination and assessment role which some felt the Council had abandoned.

In the autumn of 1974, the United Way ordered a study of the Council to be done, and hired Henry Stubbins, a man with extensive experience working in Funds and Councils in eastern Canada, to do the study:

> The desire for the study arose when several members of the Board of the United Way of Edmonton and Area were approached by citizen donors expressing their concern regarding some of the activities of the Edmonton Social Planning Council and questioned whether or not the United Way should be funding this agency.(Stubbins, Report of Study on Edmonton Social Planning Council and United Way of Edmonton and Area Relationships, 1974)

Stubbins read Council studies and consulted with Council staff, Board members, and selected people from the community, primarily from United Way agencies. He was impressed with the quality of the Council's research work and its level of support to community groups, but pointed out that the Council's insistence on maintaining a high profile in areas not of direct concern to the United Way created problems for the United Way in the reactions of its business contributors. In addition, he noted "There seems to be a lack of clarity between the United Way's own planning function and that of the Social Planning Council" (Stubbins, 1974). His report recommended that the United Way continue its core funding to the Council, but suggested a number of conditions which might be placed on the organization. These conditions included the restructuring of the Co-ordinating Committee into a traditional Board of Directors with broader representation from business, labour, and established agencies, and the prohibiting of paid staff from sitting as voting Board members.

In fact, over the three years of its existence, the Co-ordinating Committee with its three co-chairs had become less and less convinced of its effectiveness. Initially, it had seemed to work well, but its operation depended on an enormous contribution by the volunteer Committee members. Throughout the period, the committee met at least every two weeks, often once a week. In addition, many of the volunteer Committee members as well as staff worked on the Commissions and the Task Forces. The volunteers were essentially continuing the practice of the late sixties and early seventies of acting as staff in all ways but salary. However, over the three years, volunteer energy waned, and the Council had made several adjustments of the system, such that the final move back to a Board and Executive, made at the 1974 Annual Meeting, was not a major change. On the other hand, staff and most Board members liked including the staff as voting members, but had no real choice but to eliminate this practice.

Neither the United Way nor the Council were content with the remainder of Stubbins' conditions. A committee of three members from each organization was set up to arrive at a satisfactory arrangement. Roger Soderstrom, a member of that committee, reported in his thesis on the final recommendations and describes the effect of these recommendations on the Council's status:

> . . . the Committee made the following recommendations which were approved by the Board of the United Way. They are:
> a) That the Social Planning Council exist in its own right as an organization separate from the United Way.
> b) That the United Way accept the responsibility for the area of social planning which they feel is their responsibility. How

this planning is carried out is the responsibility of the Board of Directors of the United Way, and

c) That the Social Planning Council should be funded under the same guidelines and procedures as any other agency which is supported by the United Way.

The acceptance by the United Way of the Social Planning Council as just another private agency in the community marks the conclusion of a struggle between the United Way and the Council. It confirmed for the Edmonton Council an independent role enjoyed by no other Council in Canada. It confirms for the United Way its role in co-ordinating and planning for the private agencies in Edmonton. It recognizes the ideological and philosophical differences which have existed for many more years than the current conflict. (Soderstrom, p. 82)

As Soderstrom suggested, the agreements made in 1975 did confirm the Council's independence. They did not, unfortunately, confirm secure funding for the Council nor agreement by the United Way that all of the Council's activities were worth supporting. For the next five years, the Board of Directors spent much of their time struggling to find money to keep the Council afloat.

At the same time as these studies and struggles with the United Way were taking place, both staff and Co-ordinating Committee were becoming disheartened by the relative lack of impact of the various Task Force and Commission reports, despite the quality of those reports. The Annual Report of 1974 indicates a "subtle" change of the working focus:

. . . the Task Forces have successfully raised issues and provided input to all levels of government. In some cases, however, it was found that the impact of the Task Force reports might have been greater had they been presented by citizen groups prepared to *continue* working on an issue, without the further assistance of the Council.

Therefore the focus shifts — with the Council acting as consultant to citizen groups, the groups presenting their proposals to government or other public bodies, as they see fit, with no attempt to channel such proposals through Edmonton Social Planning Council Task Forces.

. . . Accordingly, it was determined to establish as the first priority,

(A) consultation to neighbourhood groups, and as the second (B) consultation to women's groups. (Annual Report, 1974)

The Council had not by any means abandoned its role of working with community groups while it concentrated on the Task Forces and Commissions; it had simply de-emphasized that role. In 1974, particularly, there had been several requests from groups such as the Oliver Social Action Committee and the Garneau Community for assistance with their research. The Council had also helped bring together a number of neighbourhood groups to form the Alliance of Neighbourhood Groups, in the hope that these groups could provide mutual assistance. In addition, the City Planning Department had contracted with the Council to provide a public awareness campaign for the Neighbourhood Improvement Program (NIP) which the federal government was funding. Missy Parnell was hired for the NIP project and also worked on the other neighbourhood projects. Deloris Russell, at the same time, was working with developing women's groups, and in the early months of 1975, researched and wrote a study of rape, *Rape: Myth or Reality*, which looked at legal, medical, and social aspects of rape and concluded with recommendations for change and self protection. By the summer of 1975, along with the changes in structure and focus, the Council had experienced a complete staff changeover and the new staff had been hired specifically to carry out the consultation-to-groups function.

Elwood Springman, first of the new staff to be hired, had an M.SW. from the University of Calgary with a major in Community Development and Community Organization. He had worked for a summer with the Hamilton Social Planning Council while taking his undergraduate degree in sociology. At the time of his application to the Edmonton Council, he was employed as a Community Worker with the Edmonton Social Services Department working with groups such as West 10 and the Oliver Social Action Committee as well as with issues such as day care, community schools, and senior citizens centres. He was hired as the new Executive Director in May 1975.

The two new planners, hired in September 1975, were Sue Arrison and Linda Duncan. Sue Arrison was a graduate from Grant MacEwan's community planning program. While working with the Council, both Roger Soderstrom and Peter Boothroyd had contracted out to teach courses in the Grant MacEwan program, and were thus familiar with Arrison as she was with the Council and its work. She was hired to work primarily on Priority A, the neighbourhood group consulting work.

Linda Duncan was a lawyer with particular interests in women's issues and environmental issues. Her immediate task was to carry on the work which Deloris Russell had begun in respect to women and rape. She worked intensively with a group of women to set up the Edmonton Rape Crisis Centre, now the Sexual Assault Centre, making funding applications to the province and city, as well as providing organizational and legal backup for the young organization. She also worked with the newly organized Women's Place and Options for Women, training volunteers, developing a television program, "Woman's World", for cable television, and assisting with grant applications.

Sue Arrison was elected to the Executive of the Alliance of Neighbourhood Groups so worked with them both as a Board member and an ESPC consultant. In addition, she worked with many individual neighbourhood groups, particularly Oliver, where she organized the Community of Oliver Group (COG), the Garneau Community League in developing the Garneau plan, the 125th Avenue Truck Route group, and the Montrose neighbourhood. Each neighbourhood required its own particular strategy, but with the building boom of the period escalating, all of the neighbourhoods were under intense development pressure. The community work of the Council was difficult, intense, and combative:

> "I was involved in Oliver. I lived in Oliver. I worked with Lynn [Hannley] and the Oliver Group there, and we did take a hard line against city hall because literally we were fighting development after development. The only way we could do it was fight hard and use the media until we got a plan in place. Staff had been hired through the Community of Oliver Group and they took on that role.

> There were a number of projects to get the community of Oliver activated, and they worked, but they were kind of alarmist approaches. We used brochures like 'Oliver-Growing, Growing, Gone' and 'Freeways or Oliver — It's Your Choice.' We were under siege from freeways. Transportation was planning all these major roadways cutting right through [the community], and the Planning Department was allowing the high rises to go up all over. So we were fighting and it didn't win us Brownie

points at all. We went head to head with Olivia Butti. She tried everything she could to get the funding pulled from the Community League.

And we went head on with Mr. Coyne [owner who demolished an old, possibly historic, house in the neighbourhood]. We had a really good citizen participation process built in there, one I think we could be proud of. We did everything possible. We set up a process whereby we had quadrant meetings. We had quadrant coffee parties leading to quadrant meetings leading to final meetings. We had newsletters that went out to every household to involve them, and Coyne knew that. But he didn't get involved until we got to the serious part where we were asking for a moratorium on development until the [Oliver] plan was finished. The plan was becoming meaningless if we didn't get a moratorium. And then he came and spoke against it." (Interview, Sue Arrison, March 9, 1990)

The work in Oliver was typical of the intensity and passion of the work in communities. A wide variety of techniques were used to activate the communities and help them resist the development onslaught, both on large and small scale issues.

One such small issue arose in Oliver, and brought together current ESPC staff with past staff and Board members. It became known that the Le Marchand Mansion had changed hands and that the new owners were planning demolition. By this time, Lynn Hannley was running her own non-profit community resource group, Communitas; Bettie Hewes had been elected to City Council, and Joe Donahue, former president of the Council was involved on the Catholic School Board as well as working from his architectural office in the Le Marchand.

Over a ten day period, Sue Arrison and the people from COG got together with Communitas to research both the architectural and human history of the Le Marchand in the hope of having the building declared a historic site. Joe Donahue introduced them to all of the residents of the Le Marchand, most of whom were senior citizens, some of whom had lived in the building for over 20 years. Bettie Hewes contacted Horst Schmidt, provincial Minister of Culture, and a meeting was set for one hour on the next Sunday afternoon at the building.

The residents were frightened, both at the possibility of having to move and at the thought of meeting the Minister. They were also exhilarated. The women set to work baking. Everyone set to work organizing — and re-organizing. Suddenly, the residents had split into two groups, quarreling over whose apartment would be used to serve tea to the Minister. After an emergency meeting with both factions, Arrison and Hannley convinced them to have two "tea parties", and agreed they would take Schmidt to both.

When Bettie Hewes arrived with the Minister, he repeatedly insisted that he could stay only an hour. The tour began with Joe Donahue leading and making introductions. Each resident met Schmidt, giving him their stories, and occasionally, their tears. Before he left the building three hours later, Schmidt had met everyone, dined at both parties, and exchanged torte recipes with two of the older ladies. Within the week, the Le Marchand Mansion had been declared a historic site. For the moment it seemed like a clear success. Much to the dismay of all involved, it later became clear that only the facade would be preserved, while the residents would be moved out in exchange for prestigious office space. However, the process does provide an example of the way that the Council was working with a whole network of community groups and community resources at the time, while itself remaining in the background where possible.

Some communites such as Groat Estates and Riverdale used resources from within, such as architects and lawyers who lived in those neighbourhoods, only using brief consulting meetings with the Council. Others relied heavily on the Council. Montrose was one of these and illustrates another Council approach:

"We worked with Montrose, tried to revive that neighbourhood in terms of community involvement. That's when we used the theatre process. That neighbourhood was problematic in terms of community involvement because there were so many elderly people. You need a younger group to get going. It was almost dying in terms of involvement. The Community League was having real struggles . . . .

They had come to us seeking help to deal with the rendering plant. So we worked with them on that in terms of how to approach City Hall, how to deal with that issue. But the greater issue then became 'how do we protect our neighbourhood as a whole, how do we deal with this on a long-term basis?'

We said 'we can help, but first you have to get the neighbourhood behind you, start working together.' They felt they didn't even

166

have the possibilities for that given the number of people they had working for the Community League.

We had a possibility of working with Dave Barnet [University Drama Department]. He was just getting Catalyst Theatre going and he'd been working with Linda Duncan on the rape crisis centre. They'd set up a number of workshops using Catalyst Theatre to bring out the issues around women and rape. It was extremely effective, and Dave Barnet was all turned on and wanted to get into another project.

So we approached him and said we wanted to try something with community development. We were experimenting at that time with ways to get people involved. Our approach was to get people involved in their own communities rather than go out and fight their wars for them . . . .

We applied for a Canada Council grant and got it, hired the actors, and started going. We'd gone through a selection process with all the communities that were facing some kind of pressure. We chose Montrose because it seemed to be the one having the most struggles and seemed to be the biggest challenge. We talked to the Executive and they were really keen. So we hired the actors, and they did the research the way Catalyst does, and put a performance together.

We did a pre and post survey, and the project didn't prove that successful. It was successful from a media point of view and as a way to approach things, but in terms of actually motivating the community to get involved more, it didn't have, in my opinion, a major impact. But I think that was the nature of the community itself." (Arrison, March 9, 1990)

In addition to working with community groups in these ways, the Council began to use an adult education approach. They began by running a series of lunch time how-to seminars at the public library, called "Taking Part: Planning Your Community's Future", dealing with issues like understanding the new Planning Act and getting a community involved. Then, Elwood Springman, concerned that the staff complement was down by one whole staff person from the preceding year, made a proposal to the Junior League that they give the Council a year's salary for a third planner in return for training being given to some of their volunteers. The Junior League agreed to the proposal, and Mike Burns was hired as the third planner. He developed the first volunteer training program, did research, and worked with some of the more traditional Social Planning Council groups such as day care parents and senior citizens. This training of volunteers as "para-professional" community workers became an important part of the Council's work:

"The other component that we had, that may not be documented as well, is that we had a whole volunteer program. We had a bunch of people that we trained to work with us. There were quite a few women from the Junior League, Lorie McMullen, Donna Golightly, Gerry deHogg. We worked with them on a regular basis. We would have seminars with them, or sit down and share things, say the philosophy of participatory democracy and how we work towards that. We involved them in our planning sessions; we involved them in any process we were doing, and they worked alongside us. That was really helpful because it extended our work, and some of those women went on to do other things. Lorie McMullen is now Executive Director of the Planning Council out in Victoria." (Arrison, March 9, 1990)

Mike Burns got a small grant from the Edmonton Association for Continuing Education and Recreation to conduct the first training program with eight volunteers. Ardis Beaudry, a founding member of the Edmonton Women's Shelter and a Board member of the Council, decided to take the training:

"I went back there because of the training they were offering. The philosophy was to make the community aware and to do leadership training in the community so you could go out and do something [yourself] . . . . It was taking back the leadership that everyone had given away to the people they'd elected. I think they were the beginners of that philosophy that said you should be taking back some of that power. I went [to the training] partly because of my work with the Shelter, and partly because of the Catholic Women's League." (Interview, Ardis Beaudry, March 26, 1990.)

The Council was very excited about this program and saw a great potential for extending their influence without over-extending staff resources. Not everyone was enthusiastic about the program:

"I remember one time when he [Elwood Springman] presented the budget to the United Way. The Council were very proud of a program they had of recruiting volunteer women to become community development workers in neighbourhoods. I think there were four Junior Leaguers who had gone through this program and were placed in communities. I remember the chairman of the [Budget] Committee said 'Yeah, and what happened?' and there was silence. 'They were placed in a neighbourhood, we got that. Now what did they do in the neighbourhood?'

Elwood said, 'I don't know.'

After Elwood left, the chairman said 'We're really interested in outcomes, not in process.' I think that was one of the times when people began to say what the heck is the Social Planning Council doing? If they're having an impact on the community, what is it?" (Bishop, March 7, 1990)

Despite the Fund's somewhat cynical appraisal of the volunteer training program, those involved were very positive, and several trainees, such as Ardis Beaudry and Lorie McMullen, went on to provide substantial leadership to the Council and other community organizations across the country.

The Council, then, in the second half of the seventies, was engaged in consulting with neighbourhood groups and women's groups as well as volunteer education. At the same time, it was struggling with its own way of doing things. The restructured Board of Directors consisted of some people from the earlier "egalitarian" era who expected to be involved in the work of community development. Some new Board members, invited onto the Board because they represented other sectors of society and other viewpoints, however, also had different ideas on their role. These two viewpoints on the Board occasionally clashed and involved the staff as well.

Mary Lou Marino, President of the Council, in 1976 and 1977, described the back and forth struggles of Board and staff in this way:

"With the staff and Board, it was a chicken and egg situation. The Board hired staff who were interested in community development. Then the staff encouraged more involvement from those Board members interested in community development." (Interview, Mary Lou Marino, February 27, 1990)

Don Sax, President in 1978 and '79, recalled it this way:

"My sense was that for some time the Council had been kind of an advocate, and somewhat dominated by the staff. There was some tension when the Board started to make some policy decisions that seemed pretty establishment to the staff." (Interview, Donald Sax, June 7, 1990)

There was, in fact, considerable controversy within the Board as to what kind of Board it should be, a "working" Board in which Board members became active participants in the day-to-day work of the Council or a policy-setting Board which would meet once a month to set policy, approve programs, and administer the organization. The staff, with its strong community development and participatory democracy stance, strongly supported the working Board role. Others felt the dual roles of Board member and volunteer confused the lines of accountability too much. This controversy led to several Board-staff workshops facilitated by Sax, an engineer and "communicator" who had become involved with the Council in the mid-seventies.

A workshop held Saturday, January 29, 1977, was typical. It began with Sax leading the participants through an imaging exercise to visualize their picture of a Humane Urban Environment, followed by an analysis of those images by looking at them through the eyes of a person from the third world. The participants went on to list in more detail their goals in the two priority areas, Humane Urban Environment and Participatory Democracy, then to list the blocks to those goals. As well as looking at these areas at the goal level, the staff listed the projects they were working on, all participants examined plan-making strategy, techniques for developing objectives, and carried out a Board self-evaluation. Despite several workshops of this general type, the Board never became completely comfortable with itself, its role, or the overall Council role during this time:

"That's what I can remember most about the Social Planning Council: every few years we would be looking at ourselves and seeing what direction we would go in. To me, it felt like we were always looking to see if we should change, but I think it was very good that they were open enough to do that . . . .

Boards tend to get the same kinds of people together; that one never seemed to. They always had very diversified people on it which made it very interesting in one sense, but it made it take a long time to make a community out of it. It always was a very loosely-knit organization and for some people that kind of situation is very hard to work in . . . . But that [change], when I look back on it, was important. So many organizations are so structured or so dogmatic about what they do that they can never change. The Social Planning Council was always able to." (Beaudry, March 26, 1990)

As this Board struggled to become a community, it also was struggling to obtain enough funding. The United Way was gradually becoming supportive again as the Council's work became less high profile and less obviously political:

". . . the transition was to depoliticize the Council to keep it going. It needed to sort out what it was and where it was going. Since I was involved and working in social planning, I could contribute some to that process . . . . Some council members were involved in direct politics. That's not wrong, but when individual members implicated the Council [it was awkward]. It was the sort of problem Councils everywhere were running into . . . . It was fine for us to have those [political] thinkers in the Council and on the Board. But we had to harness their energy in ways that did not get us into trouble with the funders." (Marino, February 27, 1990)

At the same time, City Council's grant to the Planning Council had not increased since the days of the Youth Division. Henry Stubbins noted in his report that the Council was under-funded by the City when compared to other similar-sized cities, and that in light of the neighbourhood work which the Council did, the city should grant more funds. However, given the "fighting city hall" approach of many of the neighbourhood groups, City Council was not anxious to give more funds. In 1977, the Council undertook a major campaign of public relations with the city, including preparation of a book of newspaper clippings about the Council's achievements for each alderman.

While the grant was not increased in that particular year, the campaign did begin to bear fruit as the City turned more often to the Council to conduct the citizen participation sections of various city planning projects. There were several contracts with the city, one of the largest being the Mayor's Neighbourhood Planning Conferences, a joint project with the Federation of Community Leagues completed in 1978.

Don Sax described this work as a definite move towards working with the city establishment:

"While I was there [on the Council Board], it became a little more establishment. There were some formal arrangements made to work with the city . . . . Mayor Purves was pretty strong on citizen participation. Some of the staff were quite cynical, but the Board took it seriously. We carried out a series of meetings for him. He wanted some input." (Sax, June 3, 1990)

The purpose of these Mayor's Conferences was to bring communities together to begin to deal with their collective problems together rather than bringing them to Council, community by community. They were also an attempt by the Council,

". . . to develop responsible citizen participation. It's one thing to get citizens involved but in such a way that it's not just a great big wish list. We wanted to get people recognizing the hard decisions that City Council has to make." (Sax, June 3, 1990)

The process was considered successful by the Council, although it was noted that in future processes, more time should be spent educating both citizens and the media in terms of the process of citizen participation as well as the content of neighbourhood issues. It was also pointed out that there needed to be direct feedback from City Council as to what action the city would take as a result of the citizen input.

Within a year of the Mayor's Conferences, the Council became involved in carrying out the Citizen Participation Program for the General Municipal Plan. By then, Elwood Springman had left the Council, and Alan Shugg had been hired as Executive Director. Hope Hunter, who had been hired to replace Sue Arrison when she went on maternity leave, commented on the nature, as well as the length, of the General Plan process:

"We got involved in facilitating the public participation process for the General Plan. That was Alan Shugg who pulled in that contract. It was a big boost for the Council, a $50,000 contract which in those days was real money . . . .

We had a great big time line. We spent hours going around to different little places all over the community. I'll always remember the last workshop because we all walked out . . . . It was May, a beautiful evening, the sun was still up, and we all said 'Phew, the last one. It's over.'

It was an interesting process, something that moved the Council from looking at physical planning to a broader community development concept. It really got people to look at the trade offs. We said, 'You can't just bang on the table and say I want. I want. I want.'" (Interview, Hope Hunter, April 3, 1990)

The General Plan process continued into 1980 with an *Evaluation Report: The Edmonton General Municipal Plan - Citizen Participation Program*. As in the case of the Mayor's Conferences, this report concluded that the overall process was successful; however, it did point out three major areas which would require improvement in future citizen involvement activities. These included the importance of careful timing to keep up momentum for the public and the importance of producing planning documents which were rendered in as clear and understandable way as possible. Finally, it was noted that the program had not accomplished all that had been hoped in the area of co-operation:

This Citizen Participation Program framed specific principals for co-operation and partnership among the major participant groups in an attempt to re-direct the more traditional confrontation methods of affecting change that previously tended to operate in the city. The process, which incorporated direct interaction between planners and citizens, was successful in establishing a co-operative relationship between these two groups. Unfortunately, the Program was not successful in including elected officials in the co-operation partnership with citizens. This lack of partnership was evidenced in the Public Hearings where interaction was seen as being confrontative rather than co-operation. (*Evaluation Report: The Edmonton General Municipal Plan - Citizen Participation Program*, August 1980)

These major projects came about partly as a result of the Council's search for funding which had gone on throughout the seventies. The extent of the work in that area can be demonstrated by a comparison of the income sources at the beginning and end of the decade. In 1970, the Council received funds from only two sources, the United Way and the city, plus $342 from "sundry". In 1979, the Council received funds from the United Way, the City of Edmonton, the Edmonton Association for Continuing Education and Recreation, the Edmonton Federation of Community Leagues, from the sale of Council publications, from subletting office space, and from sundry. The funding struggle was difficult, time-consuming, and anxiety-creating for both Board and staff. At times, it was necessary to look seriously at options such as staff being laid off for periods of time or working without pay, though this eventuality was never reached. Despite the struggle, however, there were always people, on the Board, within the membership, and on staff, who were determined that the Council would not only survive, but survive and continue its work. Mary Lou Marino expressed some of that sense of determination and dedication to the organization and its goals:

"The Council was always trying to do more than it had funds to do. It was involved in many areas of importance, but it did not use an approach of writing a report and letting it sit on a shelf. People were actively involved in each issue . . . . Key people have kept it going. I fundamentally believe it's vital to have an organization that represents grassroots groups and helps them gain skills and courage to represent themselves. If we believe in the capacity of the human system to learn, then it's vital to have organizations like the Council." (Marino, February 27, 1990.)

The struggles for funding and general insecurity of the Council had, however, taken its toll, particularly on staff and staff continuity. In 1977, Elwood Springman left to take on a position with the Ontario Welfare Council. In 1978, Sue Arrison left on maternity leave, then decided to go back to university rather than return to the Council. Alan Shugg was hired as Executive Director to replace Springman, but a year later left to take a more secure job with the provincial government. Trevor Thomas, hired to replace Shugg, stayed only until December 1980. Thus, as the Council moved into a new decade, it was with insecure funding and an unsettled staff — surviving, but very much in need of some stability.

Summary

1972 - 79: Strategies for Survival

The early seventies brought a deliberate move by the Council toward a more theoretical, research-based approach to social planning and away from the frenzy of response to interest groups which had been stimulated by the community development focus of the late sixties. The new staff and Co-ordinating Committee defined four areas of interest, to be studied by Commissions: Decent Standard of Living; Humane Social Controls; Participatory Democracy; and Humane Urban Environment. Particularly, through the Humane Urban Environment Commission's work on transportation, the Council had an important influence on the future of Edmonton's traffic patterns, based on Light Rail Transit and a modest system of freeways.

At the same time as the research, report-writing, and brief-presenting work was being carried out, several of those involved with the Council, both as staff and as members, became involved in civic politics, particularly in the 1972 School Board elections. This resulted in direct rebukes from the United Community Fund, and led, more indirectly, to the founding of the Urban Reform Group by Council members and others.

As some people moved toward active politics as a route to social change, there was a change of staff and of focus within the Council. The research and report-writing approach of the Commissions was seen as less effective than had been hoped. Thus, Board and staff agreed to focus on two areas of consultative support: support to neighbourhood groups and support to women's groups. For the last half of the seventies, the Council actively and quite successfully supported neighbourhood groups in their development of community plans. By the end of the '70s, citizen participation in planning was, at least institutionally, accepted by the City of Edmonton, and the Council was contracted to do city-wide citizen participation programmes for the Mayor's Neighbourhood Planning Conferences and for the General Plan. A third important focus through this period was the training of volunteer citizen para-professionals in community planning and group organization.

Throughout this entire period, the difficulties of resolving issues between the United Way and the Council made funding insecure. At the same time, the high-profile and combative approaches to work with neighbourhood groups made it more difficult to raise funds from the City of Edmonton. Thus, finding sufficient funds to support the Council's work was a constant struggle, leading to a serious search for contract work from a variety of sources.

Section Five

1980 - 89:
Nurturing Community

Chapter Sixteen

A Relevant Middle

As Executive Director of Planned Parenthood in 1977, Cynthia (Gereluk) Lazarenko felt that her Board and staff needed education about their responsibilities and relationships. She went to the Social Planning Council for help. The Council's Board-Staff workshop did help the Planned Parenthood Society, and, important for the Council, made the link with Lazarenko. Within the year, she had joined the Planning Council Board, and become one of the major figures in nurturing the Council through the difficult period, 1978 - 81, during which time there were four different executive directors:

> "Coming from an Agency and from an Executive Director's viewpoint, I joined the Council Board with an organizational background, not a social planning background. I could be a support for the Executive Director because I had personal knowledge of how a Board needs to support its staff." (Interview, Cynthia Lazarenko, March 24, 1990)

It was a period when staff needed support and stability. The funds from the United Way were shrinking in real dollars. Staff salaries and benefits were neither competitive nor assured. In addition, the lack of continuity in executive directors made it difficult to establish optimum relationships with the other staff:

> "In the time period when I was there, the basis of most conflicts were personnel management issues. Those are a major stumbling block within any organization. They were tough times." (Interview, Hope Hunter, April 3, 1990)

Hope Hunter, having begun at the Council working with community groups and then taking over the volunteer education element of Council work, took on the job of acting Executive Director during the period of months while the Council interviewed for a new

Executive Director, after Trevor Thomas left. Thus she provided some of the needed continuity.

A number of people applied for the position, including Peter Faid, with his background in research on unemployment and a Master's degree from the London School of Economics. At first, some Board members had questions about why a person with Faid's background would be applying to the Council, but that background, along with his commitment to stay at least three years, was a deciding point in the hiring.

Peter Faid, on his side, found the whole process of the interview and hiring somewhat unusual:

"I applied for the position, and immediately went to the library to see what I could find that the Council had done. I found the things that had been done in the early seventies, like the Ted Parnell material on poverty in Alberta. I was very impressed . . . .

. . . [with its] strong emphasis on public participation when that was still a dirty word and its concern with the rights of people and particularly the social rights of people; the need to provide them with sound information about their entitlements — all nurtured by the idea that we had to have those people speaking out on their own behalf.

So I was enthusiastic when I applied. I received a call from Cynthia, who at the time was President, asking if I'd be interested in an interview. When I said I was, she indicated that they didn't have much money. So I said I'd come up [from Calgary] on the bus and stay at the YMCA.

I had an interview with Board members, and as it turned out, members of the staff. Hope was involved and Nancy [Kotani] was involved. She hadn't been a member of the staff for any more than two months, and in fact, the offer that I got the very next day — I was still in Edmonton — came from Nancy, who was to be one of my fellow staff members. So it was somewhat confusing [later] to realize that people who had been on the interviewing panel were members of the staff." (Interview, Peter Faid, April 24, 1990)

In fact, Nancy Kotani began work at the Council, December 8, 1980, the day John Lennon was shot. Though only connected to that "end-of-an-era" tragedy by timing, Kotani's hiring did symbolize a major change in Council direction. She had been hired to replace Gregg Neelin, a planner whose work focused primarily on community development. Although she came with a Masters of Social Work and Community Development, her focus of interest was on how community issues fit into larger social policy analysis. The hiring of Peter Faid solidified this change of direction from a predominantly community/neighbourhood development agency to one concerned with broader issues of social policy as well.

After stabilizing staffing, a second major thrust of Lazarenko's presidency involved trying to broaden the general membership base of the Council. The Council re-instituted organizational memberships along with individual memberships. In addition, it decided to send its publications, such as the newsletter, First Reading, automatically to members, thus giving them direct and easy access to the latest information the Council had developed. The Board attempted to broaden its own membership by recruiting potential members who represented interests in society different from those already on the Board. They particularly looked for people with business interests since that viewpoint had been less well represented during the seventies.

In addition to broadening its representation, there was a definite effort to involve Board members more actively in the organization. The return to a traditional Board of Directors in the mid-seventies had been followed by some withdrawal of Board members from involvement. The first motion that passed after Lazarenko became President was that a condition of Board membership would be membership on a Council Committee. The Committees that were set up were Personnel, Nominating, Finance, Fund-raising, Program, and Public Relations. With the exception of the Program Committee, these were administrative committees, and as such, show one difference between this era and the late sixties/seventies era when Board members were primarily involved in the social issues.

An initiative, begun in the early eighties as a way to involve Board members and general members of the Council, was the Brown Bag lunches:

"One of the things we started that year, Sue [Sue Arrison was a Board member at this time] and I and the Program Committee, was the idea of Brown Bag lunches. We'd have interesting free-flowing debates at Program Committee meetings about what the topics of those lunches should be, who would give them, and who would speak.

The Board was complaining that Board meetings were all business and not very interesting. They wanted to be on the Board to learn about social issues. So we thought, 'we'll have these Brown Bag lunches so the Board can learn.' Of course, Board members seldom came to the Brown Bag lunches. Various other people came, but not the Board members.

We put a lot of work into organizing the speakers, trying to ensure balance and not providing a platform for people to speak out on one side or another of an issue. We'd try to get both sides represented. It was a lot of fun . . . ." (Interview, Judy Padua, May 15, 1990)

The topics for these Brown Bag lunches have included 'No Place Like Home: Homelessness in Edmonton', 'From Work to Welfare: Is It Really Working?' 'Getting the Ear of Government', 'Guardianship and Advocacy', 'Mothers, Midwives and Doctor: Room for all three?', 'Child Poverty: Some proposed solutions', and 'Breadlines Then and Now: How Far Have We Come Since the Thirties?'. Successful as a way of doing public education, these Brown Bag lunches are still being held.

The major administrative problem for the Board and its new Executive Director was the problem of secure and sufficient funding. When the Council had sent a request for an added half position in applied research in its 1980 budget to the United Way, the Council's services were classified as low priority and the position was refused. This refusal, and the subsequent appeal, provided Peter Faid with a quick introduction to one of his primary tasks:

"The other thing I didn't realize when I joined the Council was how tenuous the Council was . . . but I rather quickly learned that my first responsibility was to prepare an appeal to the United Way for funding. I went to the Appeal Committee and was totally overcome with the coldness of the people we were meeting with. There was a real hostility toward us." (Faid, April 24, 1980)

For Faid, the improvement of the relationship with the United Way assumed a high priority, and he spent considerable effort both in informal and formal work with the United Way. This included serving on United Way committees whenever he was invited and working on projects which were of interest and importance to the United Way and its agencies.

As well as improving relationships with the United Way, Faid also worked toward improving Council's credibility and its relationship with government. Keith Duggan, President of the Council from 1983 through 1985, describes Faid's approach:

"I think it's fair to say that for a time the Council was synonymous with a somewhat radical view on social services and almost any issue. Today a lot of those views would be considered quite mundane, but at the time, they had a reputation of being radical. There was a generation of bureaucrats, if you will, in the provincial and municipal governments who held very traditional views and in their minds the Council was far left.

I perceived Peter's intention to be to try to move the Board and the Council into a more relevant middle, a middle that could be supported by more sides, one that would attract the support not only of the volunteer agencies and the groups we worked with, but was credible with various levels of government that we looked to for support and for work. It seems to me that was a pretty intelligent thing to do.

That then was a sort of underlying theme for the three years I was there, to attract people from all sides of the political spectrum and the various aspects of society to that [Board] table, so that whatever the issue we not only had a well rounded discussion about what the concerns might be, but we were able to tap into and influence support in all sectors of the community." (Interview, Keith Duggan, April 30, 1990)

The attempt to broaden the base and move the Council to a more 'relevant middle' position was not always easy. Bringing in Board members from different social and political viewpoints created, according to Duggan, "a fair amount of friction, . . . a fair amount of emotion at those [Board] meetings".

Equally difficult was the attempt to establish the Council's voice on issues as an important and useful voice for governments to listen to. Again, Faid's approach was to use both informal and formal avenues, getting to know senior bureaucrats within the various departments as well as applying for particular projects. The problem was, of course, that the Council took contracts from government departments, but at the same time would speak up, critically when necessary, to assess government programs and policies:

"We live in a very naive political system. I remember discussing this with Neil Webber [Minister of Social Services and Community Health]. We had sent a report [on the effects of social services cutbacks] to him and to the media, saying this is the impact of these cuts and this is how disgusting we find this and this is residual social planning of the worst kind. At the same time, we were about to do some work with the Department in the area of family violence. The two documents crossed his desk at the same time. He was reported to have said, 'Don't these people realize we don't fund our critics?'

The President of the Council at the time, Keith Duggan, and I went over to meet with Webber and discuss his response. We said, 'Surely you need this kind of information from groups even if you don't agree with them in the hopper of social policy making'. He could not be convinced of that at all; he did not see that as having any validity. He indicated that he felt we had the most open, the most democratic system of government in North America, that the system was working well, and they didn't need any input from us.

I think we've moved a little bit from there. I'd like to think that has a lot to do with the type of work the Social Planning Council had done . . . . But there is that naivete that social policy is formed without the opportunity for public input, that it's done by informing some of the members of [the government] Caucus about what you're thinking, encouraging them to go home and talk over the back fence to their neighbours about children's mental health services or day care or social allowance, and see what 'the folks' are thinking." (Faid, April 24, 1990)

When the Council commissioned T. D. Weiden & Associates, in 1987, to carry out an independent evaluation of its operation, one of the major issues examined was relationship of the Council to the community. The evaluators asked members of the Council as well as community representatives about the extent to which the Council should use a social activist approach. Ninety-three per cent of the members questioned were of the opinion that the Council should maintain or increase its activist role:

We found strong support for Council to continue in its leadership role in matters of social policy and community development, that is, to continue to assume the role of active change agent in relation to those issues. There was little support for restricting Council to the role of unbiased consultant to citizen groups, or to limit to a less direct social change agent role. (*Final Evaluation Report, 1987*)

The Report noted that there was some concern about the matter of Council's credibility, but that this concern centered on finding a balance rather than on backing away from activism:

The Council's credibility can only be enhanced if it strives for balance in selecting and formulating the issues it champions, and balance in how it chooses to animate the community and, thereby, serve as a force for social change.

It was also clear that the members strongly agreed with and supported the various positions the Council had taken. This Evaluation Report, then, suggests that the move towards a relevant middle has been a successful one in that it now has strong support for both the positions it has taken and its methods of working.

Chapter Seventeen

Advocacy and the Poor

Within the Council, the 1980s have been a period of increasing stability. The Council's work, during the same period, has focused on broad social policies, and increasingly, on advocacy.

As Alberta moved into the decade, the economy began its precipitous slide from boom to bust. Neighbourhoods, that had been under tremendous development pressure, were suddenly abandoned by the developers. Bob McKeon, President of the Council in 1982, was deeply involved in the community development of his community, Boyle Street-McCauley. He noted that economics had a lot to do with the community's future:

"The neighbourhood organized politically. It's one of the stronger neighbourhoods today. The plan came out reasonably well and has been held reasonably well.... I think our main benefit was the recession of 1982/83. The people stopped making money there so the developers just went away." (Interview, Bob McKeon, May 1, 1990)

Jobs in the oil patch, in construction, and elsewhere disappeared. From rampant development, the province moved to rampant unemployment. The province with the Heritage Trust Fund began to have fiscal problems which would eventually lead to deficit budgets just like those of other provinces. The Council's new staff and directions fit well with what was needed within the new economic climate.

Of course, no changes are instantaneous, and this change in Council direction was no exception. Under Trevor Thomas during 1980, much of the staff's work still involved responses to urban planning issues. This work included a response to the city's Draft Land Use Bylaw that suggested that the Bylaw should include principles of public participation, of broad environmental concern, of flexibility, and of heritage conservation. The period also saw the Council respond to the *Interim Report on The Form of City Government - Edmonton* as well as completing its work on the General Plan.

In addition to working on urban planning issues, the Council also carried out two major research projects which were completed in 1980. Bev Zubot, one of the three planners, carried out an assessment of the needs for sheltered industry places in Edmonton at the request of the United Way, while Jackie Gaboury was hired on contract to do a Social Service Needs Assessment for the town of Spruce Grove. In addition, the Council continued and expanded its extensive training commitment to the voluntary sector through the formalization of the Volunteer Organization Training Services (VOTS). This program, carried out primarily by Hope Hunter, continued the basic Board-Staff training, but added training in areas of planning and problem solving, program evaluation, and non-profit management.

"The Council's approach to its work in the early part of the decade was certainly an empowerment agenda, of groups and people. That's why a lot of resources were put into volunteer training, facilitating community planning, which is on the process end of things. The advocacy wasn't as developed as it became, in the sense of taking positions on things and being high-profile in the media." (McKeon, May 1, 1990)

The first major project in the area of social policy analysis was the Financing Confederation Conference held on October 14, 1981. The success of this conference helped confirm staff belief that this was an important direction:

> When we first looked at the questions of poverty and unemployment it was exploratory work trying to get a handle on what we wanted to do. We spent quite a bit of time in the early years trying to look at the issues to see how we might cope with them.

> "The very first conference we worked on was probably one of the most successful we've had, and that was called Financing Confederation. We looked at the whole question of the Established Program Funding Act and CAP [Canada Assistance Plan], funding from the feds to the provinces. I don't think we quite appreciated the enormity of the issue. But it gave us a tremendous boost of confidence in that first year to say 'Hey, we can look at these issues'.

I remember participants from Health Units in rural communities telling us how pleased they were that they had been invited and how much they learned from it. It brought home to me what a critical role the Council had to play in making complex social issues more understandable." (Faid, April 24, 1990)

The conference itself drew an impressive range of experts from all across Canada from labour, federal and provincial governments, voluntary agencies, and universities. It included major papers on such areas as taxation policy and redistribution of wealth; funding of education, health, and social services; the role of municipalities; and cutbacks and the voluntary sector. Indeed, the conference planners might be thought prescient in the way that the conference topics foreshadowed some of the issues which would become critical during the decade. The Council, during its first forty years, had been witness to and participant in the creation and adaptation of a social safety net which nurtured the Canadian community. During its fifth decade, the Council has been an independent and informed voice fighting the unraveling of that net.

In this fifth decade, there have been five main areas in the Council's work: research on government social and economic policies and their effects; research on unemployment and on alternative community economic development; research and advocacy in the social welfare field; community development work; and training and co-ordination. There has also been a steady flow of publications supporting all of these themes as well as providing basic social and economic information to the public.

Following up on the Financing Confederation Conference in 1981, the Council maintained a constant watch on economic and social policies of both federal and provincial governments. A social policy news digest was created to report to Council membership and other interested parties what social policies were being considered or passed by government and what the impacts might be on the population. Shortly after its beginnings, this became known as First Reading, now a regular newsletter of the Council, well respected for its commentary and its insert, Alberta Facts which presents detailed local information about specific social issues.

". . . having local publications like First Reading [is a valuable Council activity]. We can subscribe to journals from all over the place, but what speaks of a local reality and local issues? I was part of a group long after I left the Board of the Council that worked around Alberta Facts. It was an attempt to take local information, putting it in a highly accessible way, and then trying to get it out." (McKeon, May 1, 1990)

Issued first in October 1982, First Reading has dealt with many issues including 'Medicare: New Directions', 'The Young Offenders Act', 'Mental Health Treatment', 'Family Violence - Wife Assault', 'Family Violence-Child Abuse', 'Welfare Rights . . . And Wrongs', 'Dollars and Conscience' — an issue devoted to the ethics of investment, 'Recycling', 'Literacy', and 'Urban Planning', to mention only a few.

In addition to these regular publications, whenever there were major changes in government policies, the Council assessed these and responded both to the government and to the public, analyzing the policies and the effects that they would have. The paper, *Unkindest Cuts*, was one of the early papers, and in the process of developing it, the Council learned techniques which would become part of its repertoire in the '80s:

"We learned from that experience how to work with a diverse group of people, how to use that group effectively to gather good information about people's circumstances. These were the agency people, who were much more in touch than we were with the living circumstances of people who were poor, who could bring us anecdotal information. We learned how critical it was to put those two things together, the factual data that said 'this is the situation. If you lower the shelter payments for people on welfare, this will be the impact in stark economic terms'. But the critical flavour was the anecdotal information we were able to collect. We learned that skill of writing reports that merged those two, the factual and statistical with the anecdotal." (Faid, April 24, 1990)

The Council continued this type of combined statistical and anecdotal research throughout the 80s. In 1986, a response, *Lifting the Veil of Silence*, was written to the federal cutback of $530 million over five years in funding for health and post-secondary education. In '86,'87, and '88, papers were written about the provincial government's moves toward privatization of social services pointing out some of the dangers of these moves both for the agencies and the clients involved.

The Council's sophistication in production of its publications grew during the '80s. It was a decade when the political climate for human services became less favourable and when cutbacks and reduction of deficits seemed to be the political values. Recognizing this, the Council Board and staff moved to make sure that the accessibility of their information was as good as the quality. As the Council moves into the 1990's, it is pursuing this element in its work, by hiring a full-time Communications Co-ordinator.

The Council also continued, right through the decade, its work in support of quality health care, both through organizational support to Friends of Medicare and through research, reports, and briefs. One of these briefs, *Health Care for Albertans: Making a Good Health Care System Better*, 1988, was presented to the Premier's Commission of Future Heath Care for Albertans, chaired by former Council President, Lou Hyndman. This brief suggested a number of community health initiatives which could have the effect of lowering health costs while shifting emphasis from ". . . an institution-based system that emphasizes curing, to a heath care system that promotes the physical, mental and social well-being of people." It is already clear in early 1990, with the Council's response to Hyndman's Rainbow Report, that analyzing health policy will continue to be a major concern for the Council as it moves into its second half century.

A second major theme of the Council work through the 1980s has been work on unemployment. This work, begun in 1983 has taken several forms, starting with research:

"With respect to unemployment, I felt that we needed to be a good resource for others in the community . . . . We did a major study on the social and psychological impact of unemployment. The thing that impressed us was how much of the literature was bound to the 1930's. Very little of it was new . . . .

We then tried to apply that [literature review] to the situation here in Alberta. We look[ed] at some interesting statistics. We went to Mental Health Services and said, 'can you tell us all of your intake numbers by their employment status?' When they produced these numbers for us, we were able to show that a person who is unemployed is five times more likely to use mental health services than someone who is employed. Someone on social allowance is eleven times more likely to use mental health services. We noticed that despite a determined government policy to cut back the number of wards and beds in Alberta Hospital, the number of people being admitted there was going up. There was an 18% increase in the space of two years. This was seen as a prime indicator in the literature, that 18 months to two years after rising levels of unemployment, you would find that lag effect, and the burden would be coming through." (Faid, April 24, 1990)

In 1986, this was followed by a report entitled *Unemployment — Reaping the Costs*. This report looked at revenue lost to the province through such items as lost wages and lost business earnings. It found a loss of 14 billion dollars, comparable to the Heritage Trust Fund at the time. The report also looked at health indicators for five stress-related illnesses, suicides, incidents of child abuse, and noted that all of these indicators had increased.

By the time these reports were completed, the Council was moving toward more direct work with certain groups in its constituency. Board and staff felt that they had to do more in this area, in part because of the social and economic costs of unemployment on people and their families:

"... we organized a fairly large project over two years to set up support groups for the unemployed. A lot of what we learned was that this [direct service] was a thing we probably shouldn't have done in that there was a tremendous investment in time in terms of policy development. We didn't know about the delivery of services.

We did a lot of research on the impact of this particular process on people. We weren't terribly secure with the results. We found that for those whose self-esteem was low before they became involved, their self-esteem improved. Those whose self-esteem was already okay, got worse. So we're not quite sure what we see as an outcome of this." (Faid, April 24, 1990)

Along with this work on unemployment and its effects, the Council has also looked, in the eighties, at alternatives to unemployment such as community economic development. In November, 1982, the Council developed a conference "Community Profit", with the purpose of bringing together people from across western Canada to examine the possibilities of community development corporations. The

topic was one which took fire, and in fact, people came to this conference from all across Canada, from as far away as Nanaimo, Cape
Breton, and Inuvik. In 1983, the Council carried on this theme of looking at alternatives by co-sponsoring, with Communitas and the Legal
Resource Centre, a conference on Worker Co-operatives. Then in 1985,
the Council brought Robert Theobald to Edmonton for the second
time, to lead a two-day workshop, *Work for All: Changing Perceptions
in Work, Leisure, Employment and Unemployment.*
The third major area of work, and one in which the Council has
enjoyed significant success in the 1980s, is the area of welfare information dissemination and welfare advocacy. This work began with
the research on welfare cutbacks. Then, in early 1985, the Council
obtained funding from Canada Employment and Immigration to
survey social allowance recipients,

> ... to determine what areas of the system required further
> clarification. Using the responses to the survey, project workers
> would prepare a handbook explaining the system from a recipient's
> point of view. (Surviving on Welfare - A No-Frills Flight, 1986)

With these funds, the Council was able to hire a four person team
which developed a survey questionnaire through interviews with 50
non-government agencies which had contact with welfare recipients.
The questionnaires were then distributed by those same agencies, and
over 300 were completed and returned. At that time, there was a practice within Alberta Social Services and Community Health (ASSCH)
that if people did not ask for a benefit, they would not be told of it.
One of the purposes of the questionnaires, then, was to discover what
people did know.
From those questionnaires, and from other sources such as the
Alberta Social Services And Community Health Income Security
Manual, and many interviews done by the project staff, *The Other
Welfare Manual* was prepared:

> "We hired some students on a summer grant and said 'As good
> social planners we need to find out what people who use the
> system feel about the system'. So we designed a questionnaire
> that asked those questions: How do you find you are treated by
> social workers? Are you aware of these particular benefits that
> are available?

We tried to interview social workers to get their perspective on the issue and we were turned down. Some of the [Council] staff were actually physically removed from some of the offices for handing out questionnaires. We finally got [responses from] about 350 people and we wrote a report on the basis of what they told us.

We were then able to compare the [official] policy to what people had said, and were able to show the grey areas. Things were often not interpreted as the policy was written. So often, in The [Other Welfare] Manual, we will quote the report.

We were lucky when *The Other Welfare Manual* came out. It caught the right political wave. It was the year that 16 New Democrats got into the legislature and I think the government was somewhat chastened by this experience. The document hit the Minister's desk and she was reported in the newspaper as saying 'Agency does better job than own Department'. . . . It was to her credit that she saw some merit in it . . . . They insisted they wanted to buy the document from us and that they were prepared to distribute it throughout the province.

Again, this was beyond our wildest dreams. It would allow us to get information out. We had scrounged money from a Foundation to get the [first] printing done; we had a measly 7,000 copies of this book. Suddenly, we were talking in terms of 50 and 60 and 70 thousand copies of this being printed. So this was a major success story for us." (Faid, April 24, 1990)

In the process of developing *The Other Welfare Manual*, project staff found themselves involved in a good deal of individual advocacy work. In addition, Peter Faid had looked at studies done on welfare appeals that indicated the efficacy of welfare advocacy.

"I felt there was a need for some sort of system where people could be trained as advocates. So we then decided that the next stage was to organize some sort of workshop for people to be trained as advocates to advocate on their own behalf or on behalf of others.

We had a person involved who was very experienced, having gone through the system herself from the point of view of a client. She knew the system well. With her help and the help of other staff, we developed a two day training workshop to try to help people focus on what were the critical issues of being an advocate . . . ." (Faid, April 24, 1990)

Margaret Duncan, hired in 1988, took over the work of developing the welfare advocacy when she started:

"When I came, the Council had already written *The Other Welfare Manual* and developed a welfare advocacy training workshop. My assignment was to take this project and continue to develop it. One of the things [done], was to develop a network of people who have attended the workshop. We started that in July, 1988. It's [composed of] front-line advocates who get together and share information about programs and what works and what doesn't.

I also discovered that people who receive social allowance were not registering in large numbers to come the workshops that were open to the general public. So, also in 1988, I started doing special workshops for people receiving social allowance. We've done that primarily through the Food Bank . . . . That's worked out very well. We found that people on social allowance do come when they know it's especially for them." (Interview, Margaret Duncan, June 6, 1990)

This area of welfare advocacy is continuing to expand. The Council is an active member of the Income Security Action Committee (ISAC), an interagency group that addresses issues related to income security. ISAC is involved in public education and advocacy involving Social Allowance rates, the working poor and employment programs. Other matters of concern to the committee include 16 and 17 year olds who have difficulty accessing Social Allowance programmes and the distinction made between employable and unemployable recipients. ISAC is continuing its efforts to establish and maintain communication links with government officials, both elected and non-elected.

The Community Advocates Network (CAN), a network of welfare advocates formed in 1988, has now gone beyond looking at Social Allowance to working on a variety of income support programmes such as Workers' Compensation and the Canadian Pension Plan. It is independent of the Council though still supported by Council staff, the newest Council planner, Jennifer Hyndman.

At the same time, the Council is pursuing the direction of self-help advocacy by supporting the formation of Albertans in Poverty, a group made up of income support recipients. Another new direction of the Council's advocacy work is advocacy training for the provincial welfare workers. A pilot training session was done in 1989 with Supervisors within the Social Services Department, and it is expected that in the '90s, the Council will be invited to do such sessions with the Social Allowance workers themselves.

While community development work has not been as central to the Council of the eighties as has advocacy work, there has been some interesting experimentation in this fourth area of Council work, in particular a project with senior citizens done in 1982. The Council on Aging had received a Health and Welfare grant to do some work to investigate whether or not a traditional community development approach could work with both urban and rural communities of senior citizens. The Council staff, in particular, Nancy Kotani, convinced them to try an experiment to see if it was possible to do organizing on a city-wide basis, using the media to identify and involve people in the process:

"We agreed to become the catalyst in Edmonton. What we set up was a thing called "Input - Seniors Talking To Seniors". We worked through Shaw Cable and had a Community Committee of Seniors which we had recruited through an article in the paper.

They produced a series of four hour-long shows on issues that Seniors had identified as important: aging, housing, and money." (Kotani, May 14, 1990)

One of the interesting aspects about this media-based community development was that the specific topics did come directly from the seniors. While their topics concerned the areas such as housing which most people expect will concern seniors, the particular aspects of these topics that the seniors chose were significant. For example, the topic of housing was explored under the heading 'Your Space and Mine: How to live with your kids' while another important topic was called 'Three to Get Ready' and outlined the most important three steps one should take before death.

The other important aspect of this project was the way that the television medium was used to bring people and their ideas together, people who are often isolated from other kinds of interaction:

"A group of people put together little vignettes to frame the discussion. We had studio guests. Ron Collister hosted the series, and we established a model viewing station. This was before The Journal [CBC] did all of these sort of links. We had a group of people we had recruited to view the show and talk to the guests from an on-location position.

In addition, we organized about twenty viewing stations in individual homes and senior centres where we had trained volunteer discussion leaders. People would get together, discuss the show, phone their comments in to Collister. He might deal with them on that program or have the viewing station material summarized and brought back the next week. We also had an open line link so that anyone who wasn't involved in a viewing station could also participate in the discussion.

It was an interesting way of looking at how you get people to talk about things that affect them in a way that follows the way people [usually] get information. We weren't asking people to come to a Town Hall meeting or anything like that. We were trying to get a sense whether this was a viable way to have people participate in thinking about some of the issues they're interested in, articulating them, and then having other people know about it." (Kotani, May 14, 1990)

The Council did engage in other community development activities, including holding a "Nurturing Community" conference in 1987 which examined issues such as the ethics of community development, and then presented fifteen workshops on contemporary examples of community development projects. The purpose of the conference was "to present community development as a progressive, change-oriented process" (Nurturing Community brochure) in a way that would draw in a wide range of workers from as broad a community of interests as possible.

The final major area of Council work in the eighties has been training and co-ordination. One group which received considerable benefit from this was the non-profit day cares:

"We were asked if we would convene a meeting of people from Boards of Directors from the non-profit day care centres. The person who approached us was concerned that the city was considering cutting funds [and] that the centres were not at all prepared or knowledgeable about lobbying.

So we organized a meeting. We had an incredible turnout — over 200 people from the Boards of the 13 non-profit centres in the city. What they decided to do was form an organization, so the Council got started a coalition called the Edmonton Coalition for Quality Child Care. We poured much energy and time into that thing . . . . trying to start a coalition from scratch. . . ." (Padua, May 15, 1990)

The Council continued, through the eighties, to do considerable work in researching day care standards, quality of after-school care, and the effects of poverty on children. In fact, child poverty has become a major issue for the Council, and is another issue where work is continuing into the 1990s.

"We got involved [in 1989] with Edmonton City Centre Church Corporation and a number of schools around town who were participating in a snack program. We helped to organize a conference held in May, 1989, to highlight some of the issues. We had great attendance, 180 people came to the conference.

Peter [Faid] gave the opening address, and in the afternoon, we asked people to talk about what they thought some of the problems were, what they thought some of the solutions might be, and who might be interested in following up and doing some work. We got about fifty people who said they'd be interested in doing some work. So, in September, we called a meeting, along with the City Centre Church Corporation, to do some planning. We have three committees now, and decided to call ourselves the Child Poverty Action Group. I'm the co-convenor of that group, and chair one of the committees, which is the HeadStart pre-school committee." (Duncan, June 6, 1990)

It is interesting to note that the Council was involved in the beginning of the very first HeadStart programme in the city during the sixties.

This ability of the Council to act as a leader co-ordinating agencies and other groups to work together on issues has been important in several other instances in the eighties. Throughout the decade, for example, it has been involved in bringing people together around the needs of youth. As early as 1983, it had helped create the Child and

Youth Services Co-operative which by 1990 had become the Edmonton Interagency Youth Services Association, an organization of all agencies interested in youth, a kind of '90s parallel to the Youth Services Division of the late '50s.

Another type of co-ordination begun by the Council in the late '80s has been the statistical analysis of social trends. Working together with the United Way, the Board of Health, the Regional Office of Family and Social Services, the Edmonton Community and Family Services, and the Mental Health Services of Alberta, the Council has put together a new type of research document, Tracking the Trends, which takes a particular social group and presents general economic and social statistics concerning the group and its current and future needs. The first of these documents looked at both youth and seniors, while the second, issued in the summer of 1990, deals with families with children. It is expected that this type of research, developed for the use of others, will be a continued emphasis of Council work through the '90s.

In addition, to these five major areas highlighted in the Council work, there have been several other projects. For example, in 1985, the Council was involved in organizing a foodbank convention. Since then, the Council has continued to be very active in working with food issues, having recently supported the development of the Food Policy Council, an organization that will begin to look at the crucial question of what we can do to ensure that people in Alberta have food. Another project of the Council's, carried out in 1985 by Thomas Grauman, was a series of training sessions in the area of suicide prevention. The Council has also done several research studies of social services for other communities including West Jasper Place, Lethbridge, and Lakeland. In conjunction with the United Way, the Council has carried out agency evaluations and need assessment surveys, and in 1988 produced a needs assessment workbook, Doing It Right, to assist agencies in doing their own assessments as a way of guiding their work.

The Council, then, continued through the eighties to re-organize and enhance its own organization to fit the increasingly difficult social climate, and to pursue, in particular, matters of poverty, unemployment, and social policy. As it stands poised at the beginning of its second half-century of operation, it is clear that the Council will be increasing its emphasis on human service advocacy, continuing its work on issues of poverty, particularly child poverty, and pursuing new directions in both issues and techniques.

One of the new directions which the Council has already begun pursuing is Charter of Rights and Freedoms challenges. At the beginning of the nineties, the Council is involved in researching two potential Charter challenges; one refers to discrimination on the grounds of age against 16 and 17 year olds in respect to obtaining Social Allowance and the other involves single and divorced men and women over the age of 55 who are not currently eligible for the Widows' Pension Plan and Spouses' Allowance.

The future of the Council in the nineties, then, would seem to be one of continuing current directions, and developing new approaches to those issues identified as most crucial as the decade unfolds. Whatever the issues are, the current governing philosophy of the Council will no doubt continue to direct Council action as it proceeds. That philosophy is perhaps best expressed by Harvey Krahn, President of the Council in 1988:

"It is a commitment to social justice in the broad sense of the word, recognizing that the community — again broadly defined — is more than just business enterprises and formal organizations, but that in fact there are people and families and groups that may not always have the quality of life that one would like for everyone. I think that kind of belief that things could be better for individuals and families and community groups probably is the underlying belief that attracts Board members and staff members to the Council." (Interview, Harvey Krahn, March 6, 1990)

Chapter Eighteen

A Wealth of Voices

Tuesday evening, June 27, 1939, representatives of 50 social agencies voted to create the Edmonton Council of Social Agencies. **"This is a great day for Edmonton,"** enthused John Blue of the Chamber of Commerce. Fifty years later, it is clear that the Edmonton Social Planning Council has lived up to the expectations of that evening.

There have been, of course, many changes in the Council in that fifty years: changes of name, of formal Objects, of staff, of structure, and philosophy. Beneath the surface of these changes, however, it is possible to see a strong core of belief in social justice for all that has been the motivating principle throughout.

The very first Council constitution included as one of the Council Objects, 'To facilitate concerted action in matters of social reform and the development of public opinion on social problems'. While the language has changed and the view of social reform has, perhaps, enlarged, the continuity between that Object and the Council's current Mission Statement, adopted in 1987, is apparent:

> The Edmonton Social Planning Council believes that all people should have the social rights and freedoms to live and work in an environment that enhances individual, family, and community growth without restricting the same rights and freedoms for others. The Council seeks to create, to advocate, and to support changes in policies, attitudes, and actions in order to enhance these social rights and freedoms.

While the motivating principles and aims have shown remarkable continuity over the fifty years, the voices with which the Council has spoken have changed according to the times, the attitudes of the society, the urgency of the needs, and sometimes, according to the personalities of the leaders within the Council. It began as the voice of the social agencies, of the professional social workers who were just starting to become a force in Alberta society. It was a voice that urged increasing skills for the care-takers, increasing standards of care for the disadvantaged. This voice of the Council's is, of course, still heard, as social workers within Alberta struggle for improved conditions for their clients and themselves.

As Edmonton grew, and the dominant views in that society began to change, the Council's concept of its constituency, and thus its voice, adapted to the needs and thinking of that constituency. The voices of community leagues, departments of the university, of service clubs, of particular groups in society such as seniors and immigrants merged into the vocal chorus of the Council. During the sixties and seventies, the voice expanded dramatically. The voices of the disadvantaged themselves now spoke through the Council. These were sometimes strident voices, expressing the frustration, and even rage, born of years of not being heard. In the eighties, the voice has become quieter, but no less insistent, carrying its message of social justice to perhaps the broadest audience of its history.

The issues that have concerned the Council have, throughout its existence, been the central issues of human well-being: the issues of equity and access to that which our society offers; issues of prevention of any kind of human pain rather than its after-the-fact correction; the issues of democracy, freedom of choice, access to information, access to power within a democratic system. Michael Phair, President of the Council in 1989 and '90, expresses his view of the Council's strength in presenting these issues:

". . . on the broad perspective [the Council's important strength] is similar now to what it's been through the history of the organization. [It is the ability to] step outside the day-to-day business of what's going on and take an analytical look to see what it means and what needs to be done; the ability to step back and view the larger picture . . . .

The second significant area is the collaborative effort, of working with and being part of directions that pull together a group of people, acting as a kind of catalyst, facilitating movement on issues." (Interview, Michael Phair, June 13, 1990)

These abilities to analyze the larger picture and to bring together a variety of people and organizations to work on issues have been used on a broad range of particular issues: work with youth began in the forties and has continued through the entire history; concerns about housing, about health, about services for children and for seniors were also first raised in the forties, and were raised again during each decade, although the level of understanding of the needs has changed as has the type of services required as the complication of our society has increased. Work with transients and the unemployed began to become crucial during the fifties while native issues were first dealt with by the Council in the early sixties. In the process of working on these issues, the Council has been involved in the founding of many of the community organizations that are now an integral part of Edmonton, such as the Community Chest-United Way and the Christmas Bureau begun in the early forties, the Boyle Street Co-op, social service departments in hospitals, the John Howard Society and the Retired and Semi-Retired, the Community Connections service and the Women's Shelter

Indeed, the range of the issues in which it is concerned has always been a problem, in that Council staff, volunteers, and resources have never been able to stretch as far as the concerns. Thus, these issues have never been dealt with all at one time. It is easy to see, however, that they return, almost cyclically, to the front of the Council agenda as the prevailing social and political attitudes change. In the broadest sense, it can be said that throughout its history, Council has participated in the ongoing debate about where the responsibility for human services lies; with government and the taxpayer; with voluntary services; with the individual him or herself. From the forties until well into the seventies, the national mood was one of accepting more and more responsibility through government for the welfare of the people. In the eighties, the mood has turned considerably, as governments cut social, health, and education dollars, and move whenever possible toward privatizing services. The Council can be counted on, in the face of these attitudes, to be speaking out on behalf of the disadvantaged, but also to be looking for new ways for the voluntary sector to work to increase the efficacy of the resources available.

Thus today, in 1990, the foremost issue for the Council is poverty — child poverty, poverty and the continuing need for social assistance and the other elements of the social safety net. Already however, the Board is also contemplating some return to looking at the issues of city planning. Jan Reimer, Edmonton's mayor and former Planning Council Board member, challenged the Council at its Annual Meeting, in March 1990, to make itself heard on urban issues:

City hall needs help in maintaining the political will to turn the verbal commitment to inner-city neighbourhoods into action, she said.

"Your voices are needed — and I need to hear them."

Jan Reimer, quoted in First Reading, May/June 1990)
Already, it should be noted, the May/June 1990 issue of First Reading was devoted to urban planning — the Council's voice is being raised on this issue once again.

Speaking out in this way on behalf of the disadvantaged, whether for an inner city neighbourhood or a rebellious youth, is not always welcomed in our society, especially by those who do enjoy the advantages available. The Council, nevertheless, has survived, despite often being a controversial voice, speaking of uncomfortable issues, sometimes just ahead of the general recognition of those issues. This leads to the question of how the Council did survive these fifty years, especially when so many similar organizations, including many planning councils, have disappeared.

One part of that answer may be found in the relationship of the Council to the Community Chest, and later, to the United Way. The relationship of any social critic with a funder, usually a funder from the more established sectors of society, is inevitably going to be volatile. For this Council, it seems that the relationship with the Chest or United Way has become difficult, and consequently been re-examined, at least once every decade. At times, there have been serious questions from the funder as to the value of most Council activities. These questions have often led the Council into intensive periods of introspection on its own idea. Ultimately, however, its activities have been guided by the idealism and intelligence of those involved with the Council. Thus, once explained with clarity to the United Way and other critics, those activities have always found enough support to continue.

This also points to the wealth of human leadership within the Council: the staff, volunteers, and Board members that the Council has always attracted. In a circular way, the value of Council activities has attracted valuable people whose determination, dedication, and courage to innovate has, in turn, supported those activities. From the very beginning, the Council attracted many people whose interests lay with public life. Cora Casselman and Elmer Roper, from the first Executive Committee, went almost immediately into politics. Marcel Lambert was Vice-President of the Council when he was first elected to Ottawa in 1957. Lou Hyndman, David King, Gerry Wright, Bettie Hewes, Jan Reimer have all been involved with the Council, which both benefited from their work and acted as a training ground for their future work:

"I would never have made it into public life if it hadn't been for the Council. The Council provoked me to do some stuff with the City, provoked me to get on the Parks Board. The Council had collaborated with the Community Planning Association of Canada, way back when, on preservation of the river valley. It was during one of those when I was ranting on that Elmer Roper, who was the Mayor, needed somebody to go on the Parks Board and wanted a woman, so put me on. Eventually I became Chairman . . . ." (Hewes, February 5, 1989)

As well as being a source of political leadership, the Council has been the benefactor of much leadership from the university and colleges. Similarly, many of those involved over the years have gone on to university and college careers. Bill Nicholls points out that all of the staff and some of the volunteers from his era went on to future careers in teaching some aspect of the social science curriculum in university, as did people like Leslie Bella and Peter Boothroyd from the seventies.

Other 'alumni' who honed their skills and understanding at the Council have gone on to other social service activities. Gustave deCocq became Executive Director of the Calgary Social Planning Council; Elwood Springman moved to the Ontario Welfare Council; both Hazeldine Bishop and Jack Anguish moved to the London Council of Community Services while Lori McMullen became Executive Director of the Victoria Community Council. David Critchley, after a stint at university teaching, returned to his home in Bermuda and became Deputy Minister of Social Services there.

Locally, Hope Hunter became Executive Director of the Boyle Street Co-op while Nancy Kotani moved to the Edmonton Board of Health to become involved in health promotion. Sue Arrison followed the political route developed through URGE and now works as an assistant to Mayor Jan Reimer. She remembers the Council as a place where her ideals were confirmed as valid:

"For me, the Council was the one job that was in tune with my value set more than any other job I've ever had. It helped to reinforce things that I was formulating in my own mind and put them into practice and see the realities of that. I think it was really a tremendous growth experience. I was really naive when I went into that job, but what I realized is that it is possible to be an idealist. The Council showed that you can actually work toward ideals and make it happen." (Arrison, March 9, 1990)

Lynn Hannley, another former Council staff, started her own community resource organization, Communitas, and has, for seventeen years developed co-operative housing in Edmonton and fostered the co-operative housing movement across Canada. Her recollection of the Council's influence on her is a recollection of the people:

"What was important for me was the people I worked with, like Bettie [Hewes], like Joe [Donahue], George [McDermott], Marc [Barrier], Marsha [Mitchell]. It was part of a walk-through of life — you learn a lot. It was a meeting place." (Hannley, March 7, 1990)

Leslie Bella and Keith Duggan, both Presidents of the Council at one time, saw the Council as a place where they were not only able to work toward things that they saw as important, but where they learned about society and tried out valuable leadership skills for themselves:

"It exposed me more intimately to people and issues in the social services realm and the human needs and human issues realm, particularly the volunteer sector part of it.

It gave me a valuable opportunity to develop and apply skills that my own profession couldn't give me in areas like budgeting, lobbying, chairing of diverse organizations, program design and management, selection of staff, and solicitation of Board members." (Duggan, April 30, 1990)

There are, in fact, hundreds of people living in Edmonton and across the country who have, in one way or another, contributed through the Council, and later in an amazing range of ways, to the fabric of our society. It is the idealism, struggle, innovation, and determination of these people which has created the Edmonton Social Planning Council while the organization gave ideas, skills, and contacts back to those people. It is not enough when looking at the Council to tally up its achievements in terms of briefs written or agencies started; it is the human wealth represented by the many voices of the Council over the years which is its major legacy.